I0811407

A LIFE OF ILL REPUTE

A Life of Ill Repute

Public Prostitution in the Middle Ages

MARIA SERENA MAZZI

Translated by Joyce Myerson

McGill-Queen's University Press
Montreal & Kingston • London • Chicago

© McGill-Queen's University Press 2020
Originally published in 2018 as *La mala vita: Donne pubbliche nel Medioevo* by Societa editrice il Mulino, Bologna

ISBN 978-0-2280-0153-9 (cloth)
ISBN 978-0-2280-0154-6 (paper)
ISBN 978-0-2280-0208-6 (ePDF)
ISBN 978-0-2280-0209-3 (ePUB)

Legal deposit first quarter 2020
Bibliothèque nationale du Québec

Printed in Canada on acid-free paper that is 100% ancient forest free (100% post-consumer recycled), processed chlorine free

The translation of this work has been funded by SEPS
Segretariato Europeo per le Pubblicazioni Scientifiche

SEPS
SEGRETARIATO EUROPEO PER LE PUBBLICAZIONI SCIENTIFICHE

Via Val d'Aposa 7 – 40123 Bologna – Italy
seps@seps.it – www.seps.it

Funded by the Government of Canada | Financé par le gouvernement du Canada | Canada | Canada Council for the Arts | Conseil des arts du Canada

We acknowledge the support of the Canada Council for the Arts.
Nous remercions le Conseil des arts du Canada de son soutien.

Library and Archives Canada Cataloguing in Publication

Title: A life of ill repute : public prostitution in the Middle Ages / Maria Serena Mazzi.
Other titles: Mala vita. English
Names: Mazzi, Maria Serena, author.
Description: Translation of: La mala vita: donne publiche nel Medioevo. | Includes bibliographical references.
Identifiers: Canadiana (print) 20190223464 | Canadiana (ebook) 2019022351o | ISBN 9780228001539 (hardcover) | ISBN 9780228001546 (softcover) | ISBN 9780228002086 (PDF) | ISBN 9780228002093 (EPUB)
Subjects: LCSH: Prostitution—History—To 1500. | LCSH: Prostitution—Social aspects—History—To 1500. | LCSH: Prostitutes—History—To 1500.
Classification: LCC HQ115 .M3913 2020 | DDC 306.7409/02—dc23

This book was typeset by True to Type in 11/14 Sabon

Contents

Preface

Why does a woman sell her body? Medieval lawmakers would have answered that she does it "*Pro pretio* (in exchange for a price), *lucro* (profit) *et questu* (and solicitation)." The official wording defines the activity of a public prostitute and the terms of the transaction: "*corpus suum libidini praebet pro pretio, lucro et questu*" (she lends her body out of lust in exchange for a price, for profit, and solicitation). The price established the value of the merchandise, the profit represented material advantage received from the transaction, and the *questua* pointed to the specific request for money in exchange for sexual commerce or, one could say, the act of begging. The essence of the exchange lay in the economic transaction, in the handover of money. Promiscuity, another defining characteristic, resided in the background – implicit and taken for granted.

These words, however, were used to indicate only some characteristics of prostitution: specifically the commercialization of the act, an essential component for public authorities to identify the females involved so as to subject them to special rules and restrictions. They do not explain how and why one became a prostitute or endured this way of earning a living – a method one might have difficulty calling work or a profession, as it is sometimes labelled, and that entailed a pattern of existence engulfing all of one's life, relationships, self-esteem, religious beliefs, morality, and social position. What could make someone put her body up for sale? Was it the absolute absence of means, the lack of an alternative occupation, of a family, some violence suffered, or the result of some war? Or was there at play some choice made in the name of independence and freedom, in the conviction that one could live more comfortably, wear more elegant clothing, eat better, derive desirable material benefits that compelled some to practice prostitution? Or could this person have been coerced by someone, a family member or a stranger? Was she a victim of blackmail, deception, or the scheming of traffickers? Was the woman in question thinking it was a temporary choice or was she aware that it represented an irreversible turning point in her very existence?

Whatever the motivation and individual awareness, prostitution was an uncomfortable reality. The activity and people involved created discomfort. Both the enterprise itself and the women engaged in it embodied a complex and widespread phenomenon and, most of all, a problem that was difficult to contain, let alone resolve. Throughout the centuries there have been numerous attempts to contain or solve the issue, some apathetically and half-heartedly proposed in the wake of a scandal or protest, others in an urgency to rehabilitate or sudden eagerness to moralize. Despite those efforts, prostitution remains concealed and persistent, something unchangeable – a legacy from the past, a remnant of distant origin, ingrained, innate, and ineradicable.

Long after the Middle Ages, we still prefer to ignore, overlook, distort, or hint at prostitution with winks, nudges, and allusions, and, above all, choose to keep silent and not name or give weight to the phenomenon and its history. In doing so, we fail to recognize a reality that is malleable, one with which we may come to terms, both in the past and in the present. Amid fleeting episodes of condemnation and upheaval are interspersed situations filled with awkward silences, indifference, complicity, inertia, whitewashing, or noncritical approval supported by medieval concepts of the naturalness of instincts and the need to satisfy them. After all, don't we still name prostitution with the grotesque and commonplace phrase, uttered with the undisguised smugness of someone in the know, as the "oldest profession in the world"? On the evidence of so many generations, it appears that we can't get rid of it, and who wants to anyway? Isn't it true, moreover, that the endurance of the phenomenon implies that we can't do without it, and, therefore, it would be useless to try? Is there, in fact, any reason to revolutionize a centuries-old practice?

And is it worth drawing attention to the documents and the evidence of the phenomenon throughout time? Should we allow prostitution to become the object of an historical investigation instead of a mere object of simplistic and provocative curiosity? Perhaps we wish to ignore the infinite connections to our economic and social organization, culture, gender relations, moral code, and concepts of sexuality. It is an issue that is unseemly and inconvenient, one to be passed over in silence, and kept out of sight. Besides, the research is difficult to conduct, the books troublesome to write, and slightly tainted with indecency. According to the opinion of some, they are even difficult to come by and especially to exhibit, whether on bookstore shelves or in living rooms. Such a book would scandalize guests, as one self-righteous woman recently proclaimed at a social event.

PART ONE

The Words for It

I

"Using One's Body for Ill-Gotten Gain"

Behind us we have ten centuries of reflection, questions, and proposals on the issue of prostitution. Throughout that time we have made decisions, then renounced or dismantled them, only to start from scratch again – goals have been pursued, reasons formed to condemn those goals, and repudiations raised against the reasons to condemn. We have simultaneously censured and sanctioned, and over and over again we have admitted defeat. The troublesome and embarrassing presence of prostitutes within the cycle of medieval daily life remained an unsolved problem and a source of unease for the community then while remaining a complicated knot right into our own time. Unfortunately the history of failures, attempts at solutions, and the constant debates have not been passed down to us together with a legacy of experiences and teachings of which we can make use.

This issue, which legislators, politicians, philosophers, and thinkers, as well as the clergy, have slaved and sweated over, has always entailed one basic characteristic: ambiguity. In medieval Western societies, prostitution was considered a disgrace and the prostitute an indecent woman to be relegated to the margins of community life, a fallen woman, irredeemable unless she went through processes of repentance and atonement. The aim of the condemnation was not necessarily to eliminate the phenomenon but rather to distance oneself from it while immediately attesting that prostitution was impossible to thwart. To censure and justify, to prohibit and accept, to repress and legalize, were the contradictory paths manoeuvred, all vain attempts to unravel the muddled tangle in which social and moral reality, religious and ethical thought, norms of behaviour, laws, and sexuality had become so tightly intertwined.

So, in the Middle Ages, in addressing the issue of prostitution, we find ambiguity coupled with a sense of professed impotence sustained by a will to inaction, except in extreme cases when it was believed that the divine was meting out punishment in the form of natural disasters, famines that stripped the very flesh off bodies, or plagues that reaped copious piles of human lives. The justification that prostitution is impossible to eradicate or resolve persists through the ages. The "world's oldest profession" is an ancient saying that suggests that the selling of one's body, in order to live or survive, simply, comfortably or in luxury, may be defined as work: the first "profession" recognized and remunerated as such. As well, many of the words used to describe prostitutes suggest that the woman was born branded with this destiny and predisposed to perform this service. As a result, we are faced with conceptual confusion, linguistic uncertainty, and a reluctance to use words of clarity. We need diverse words to define a prostitute, her existence, and her relationship with men. In this regard, medieval societies expressed great ability and meticulousness. In fact, during that time, there were many terms identifying prostitutes and giving name to the activity. Within the domain of romance languages, the dependence on Latin is obvious. The words *meretrix* (paid woman in Latin) and *prostituta* (in Italian) make a direct allusion to the act of exhibiting something, specifically a woman's body, for sale. But *prostitute* is a term that has passed into the Germanic languages and is found in English and German dictionaries. In various documents the word *meretrix* is generally associated with *ganea*, a word defining the Roman tavern, thus equating the place with the function since the activity was often undertaken within this establishment. *Mugeres erradas* (improper women), *malas de sus cuerpos* (wicked in their bodies), *mugeres del sieglo* (women of the world), *rameras* (harlots), *mujeres mondanas* (worldly women), *putas* (whores) is what they were called in Castile. In Pistoia, Italy, they were known as *donne cortese* (obliging women), *donne di partito* (common women) in the Italian cities of Arezzo and Ferrara, *mammole* (violets, which grow half-hidden at the edge of the woods or fields, paradoxically conjuring up the image of a reserved and modest girl), and then more generically as *male mulieres* (indecent women).

Instead of employing a noun or a simple adjective, sometimes it was preferable to resort to meticulously detailed and unequivocal expressions to avoid any doubt whatsoever: "women of evil life, condition, and repute," "she who makes herself carnally known now with this one, now with that one, or she who has the name and reputation of a wanton woman of indecent life,"[1] a woman "who makes her body available for carnal lust in order to receive monetary gain," or she who "publicly and blatantly commits her body indiscriminately to any and all" for money.[2] In the cities of southern France they were defined as *meretrix publica* (public prostitute), *puta* (whore), *putaine* (whore), *bagasse* (prostitute), *femmes cantonnières* (street women), *femmes lubriques* (lubricious women), *femmes dissolues* (dissolute women), *femmes déshonnêtes* (indecent women), and *filles perdues* (lost girls).[3] The obligatory references in all these are to indiscriminate promiscuity, to the offering of one's body in exchange for money to whoever asks for it and is prepared to pay, and to the willingness to satisfy the lustful cravings of all and sundry.

At least three hundred different words for prostitute have been uncovered in the literature of the sixteenth and seventeenth centuries.[4] The various designations depend in the first place on how the activity was carried out, whether unseen in private homes and as secretly as possible or publicly, as a recognized exercise conducted within the walls of officially marked brothels.

In the Kingdom of Castile the *putas publicas*, the public women, were contrasted with the *rameras*, meaning the clandestine women. In Valencia they called the former *mujeres publicas* and *mondarias* (public women) and the latter, *encubiertas* (secret women). But there existed more accurate differentiations associated with the location of the activity, where clients were solicited, a place one used for work. In the Castilian language the differences are specified in a varied repertory of phrases: the *puta de canton* was she who occupied a street corner, always the same one, which she lay claim to; the *puta callejera*, on the other hand, walked the street, soliciting the curiosity and desires of men in various locations; the *puta de posada* operated within the inns, where people ate and drank wine and were more inclined to yield to their desire for pleasure; the *puta*, a woman with a house, worked in private dwellings, not necessarily her own. Castillians also referred to the *puta de cementerio*, the woman who hid in mysterious places inhabited by the dead, as well as the prostitute of the *de albergue de pobres*, any kind of poor shelter for humanity living on the margins.[5]

Jacques Rossiaud writes that in the thirteenth or fifteenth century "from Sicily to Andalusia, from the Languedoc to Bohemia, conventional wisdom recognizes, in societies that are not too different from each other, four orders of belonging or adherence to the world of prostitution."[6] We have the public *meretrices*, the girls of the bordello and the common girls in the first group; in the second, the *cantoneras*, prostitutes of the street, square, and tavern, both public and clandestine; in the third, the lovers; in the fourth, the kept women, the more fortunate ones holding a higher position.

As for the act of prostitution, here, too, are found a diverse assortment of terms, most of which are characterized by a common sense of contempt and implicit or explicit disapproval. *Meretricare* or the "art of the public *meretrix*" appears as a neutral expression, while "using one's body immorally" or "lending out one's body immorally" contain value judgments and condemnations. *Mercimonia inhonesta* (dishonourable merchandise) and *vituperoso exercitio* (disreputable practice) also hold negative connotations while others also allude to the method of earning: *feminas facientes se conoscere* (women who make themselves known), a woman who *questum sui corporis faciens* (solicits her body), "a girl available to the desire of many men." All these are terms found in a vast body of religious texts, sermons, and public documents to do with city administration.

In daily life, when one wanted to insult a woman, one resorted most often to terms alluding to lewdness or her willingness to surrender her body for money or immoral motives that caused scandal and corrupted honest men. Indignities of this sort included "whore," "slut," "tart," "harlot," "tramp," "loose woman," "trollop," "putrid strumpet," "rotten wench," "stinking skank." Taken together, these may seem equal, but if we look carefully we may detect differences on the scale of derogatory meaning, even if in common language they were used haphazardly.[7] On a summer day in 1436, a complaint was made before the powerful Florentine magistracy, the Otto di Guardia (an eight-member entity tasked with administering some aspects of criminal justice in Renaissance Florence). A quarrel between two women had erupted, and it would have been unimportant had it not quickly escalated into a fight in which profanity was used. The protagonists were the wife of a poultry vendor and a dissatisfied client who complained of the foul smell of the meat. The latter was rewarded with various epithets in response to her remonstrations: "slave and daughter of a slave, whore and bastard daughter, shameless liar."[8] In this episode the term *puttana* (Italian for whore) figures only on the second rung of the hierarchy of insults, if we had to create a scale of social indignities. But the meaning of the word, which came to Italian via the ancient French *putain*, is complicated by its Latin root, *putidum*, namely "dirty, foul-smelling" (although not everyone agrees with this derivation). The lexicon of slurs of a sexual nature sometimes contained this "olfactory disdain,"[9] which, when linked to the *meretrix* (prostitute), becomes particularly evocative through the incorporation of additional nuance.

That dirty, foul-smelling, "putrid" body belongs to the contaminated prostitute, carnally savoured by too many men. She is a foul and corrupted corruptor, who, in her very own used and worn out limbs, symbolically expresses the slow disintegration engendered by sin and evil. The epithets evoke a revolting image brought to mind in a letter written 8 September 1509 by Niccolò Machiavelli to his famous friend Luigi Guicciardini. Machiavelli sent the letter from Verona to Guicciardini in Mantua and in it he described his encounter with a woman. He wrote of the darkness of a hovel, a house "more than half underground," with just a glimmer of feeble light that hid more than it revealed, where the writer nonetheless committed a rough, hurried, and short sexual act, "such was the desperate desire" (*foia*) that overwhelmed him. Then came the revelation. The woman – half-hidden by darkness and with a cloth concealing her face, although perceivable to some degree by her aged and withered features and by the smell emanating from her – appeared, in the reddish light of some embers, not like a woman but a "monster," partially bald, covered in lice, filthy and drooling, repulsive: "merchandise" so rotten and of such disgusting appearance that Machiavelli vomited on her, paying for the service in that way.[10] Machiavelli's frenzied intercourse, in a hovel resembling a lair, was caused, as he himself admits, by his desperate desire (*foia*). This is a strange use of a term usually referring to the desire or intense sexual excitation of animals and not persons.

Machiavelli's use of the word is perhaps reflective of what is written in the *De regimine principum* of the Dominican Thomas Aquinas, popularized by Bishop Bartholomew of Lucca, where he writes "the public woman in society is what the bilge is on a ship and the sewer in the palace. Take away the sewer and the palace becomes rank and rotten."[11] This is a terrible simile, a devastating condemnation, which reduces the bodies of women to mere instruments of garbage collection, storehouses of the liquid sludge coming from men reduced to animals that have been provoked by a single impulse, an uncontrollable drive to empty themselves of their bodily fluids, so that the entire community might escape infection – an unstoppable need to copulate that must be satisfied in order to ward off dangerous contagion. The depraved and sinful space, as well as commoditized sexuality, had to exist in medieval societies in order to allow virtue to survive. The conception of the woman as a pure virgin that must be protected, the good bride–mother able to guarantee the purity of lineage through her absolute faithfulness to her husband, encouraged the creation and preservation of the model for a different kind of woman, unchaste and wayward, to be used as a release for the unsuppressed stirrings of men.

Medieval tradition fluctuates in usage between two possible descriptions of a prostitute's activity: either the selling or the lending of her body. These appear to have been used interchangeably and without being distinguished. The constant is the exchange of money between the prostitute and her client. "Selling" implies temporariness – otherwise the acquisition would be permanent – while "lending" is a more accurate description of the act given that it involves a transitory loan. In the first instance, one might consider that what is being sold is a service of a sexual nature and therefore a "work-related" activity, while in the second, the depersonalization of the woman seems complete, as if she almost has to remove herself from her body in order to hand it over and allow others to exploit it.

And who or what decides which women are condemned for the good of others, sacrificing their bodies, depriving themselves of personal essence, alienating their bodies in order to lend them out, placing their very existence in the service of a male collective? Is it perhaps lust, often considered a typically feminine characteristic, or is it woman's nature, inclined towards lasciviousness, which leads her to sin? Or is it birth, poverty, manual labour, servitude, solitude, disgrace, war, rape, or chance that induces her to become a "bad" woman and not a respected one?

During serious famine, with no public or private resources and endless hunger, in the hope of finding food people are capable of breaking all barriers, of forgetting compassion, love, and duty to their children. A Catalonian traveller, Pero Tafur, told the story of a mother who tried to sell him her virgin daughters, choosing a stranger so as to avoid attracting the attention of her fellow citizens. Tafur was so upset by the proposal that he gave the desperate woman a substantial sum of money, demanding in exchange her promise never to repeat her act of desperation.[12] This is one way that a woman may become a prostitute and end up living in a circumscribed space, eternally repeating the same gestures, and living as a mere object and instrument of male desire. Brothel, bawdy house, bordello, whorehouse, den of iniquity, house of assignation, house of ill repute, stew, joy house, cathouse, house of prostitution are just some of the words used to define the places and structures used for the residence and activity of public women, where hard-working public functionaries and well-educated men of the government undertake to confine them with the approval of self-righteous citizens and the blessing of the church.

2

The Opinion of the Church

Through the centuries, the church's dictates regarding sexuality and sexual practice have become increasingly complex, taking on multiple layers of meaning as the original commandments are enriched, expanded upon, and adapted to more complicated types of social organization as well as the more intricate and multifunctional structure of the ecclesiastical institution. Preaching and the practice of the confession were used to disseminate regulations to the community of believers. Those regulations then became part of the life of the individual and of the collective by shaping their consciences. The tradition of penitential acts, an effective technique used by confessors, demonstrated that the church was compelled to censure an ever-growing number of infractions regarding "sins of the flesh." The church was not disposed to leave judgment up to the personal evaluation of its curates but rather required a uniformity of thought and action. The penitent, on the basis of instructions publicized as an organized compilation of issues and cases, was subjected to an exacting interrogation encompassing every one of his/her acts and thoughts.[1] In the central centuries of the Middle Ages, interrogations of this type became less frequent, but they did not disappear altogether and then regained momentum at the beginning of the sixteenth century.

Independent of the mechanism that brought it into effect, confession had great value in the formation of a morality. This minute inquisition of the individual, of his or her most jealously guarded and intimate life experiences, secret acts, and thoughts, was pursued with a scrupulousness devoid of any leniency and a passionate love for precision of information. The intention was to strip the individual's soul bare in order to enable its ultimate purification. Undoubtedly this had a highly persuasive effect on those undergoing confession. Confession also represented the believer's personal connection to religious precepts and was a powerful means for the priesthood, who safeguarded decency, to remind the faithful of church doctrine, the observance of rules, principles, and the right behaviour to uphold.[2] The church's judgment of sexual transgressions found expression in works that had widespread circulation and a considerable following. For example, the *Decretum* of Burchard of Worms, written between 1007 and 1012, was very popular in areas of the Holy Roman Empire, Germany, Italy, Lorraine, and Northern France. The author sought to enlighten readers by pointing out evil and where it hid and by suggesting what paths clerics should follow in undertaking a thorough investigation with the goal of guiding the deviant person away from evil and towards good through repentance.[3] There was a later *Decretum* by the jurist Gratian, written in 1140, which almost completely obscured the previous text by Burchard and became the basis of canonical law. Although Gratian abandoned general considerations on the control of sexual practice, he nonetheless meticulously specified periods of abstinence and explicitly condemned the "sin" of sodomy.

In the early Middle Ages, ensuring morality through the work of priests, confessors, and tracts written to clarify the church's message on sexuality, was made easier by an additional and even more popular vehicle: the sermon. The thirteenth century gave rise to the friar of the mendicant orders – a new religious figure – who was a fierce promoter of the apostolate and preaching and whose eloquence attracted a vast public that included both men and women. The great Dominican, Franciscan, and Augustinian sermons, with their didactic, illustrative, and evocative attributes, became effective modes of persuasion for masses of people who otherwise would not have been reached. The squares in front of Dominican and Franciscan monasteries filled with crowds of people eagerly listening to messages concerning social problems and recent events that were spoken in a language closer to their own. The sermons eschewed conceptual abstractions with words difficult to understand and were filled with concrete practicalities. They proposed models of virtue and provided precise, clear, and easy-to-follow directions on virtuous behaviour while discouraging bad habits with the threat of eternal damnation. Some of these were very famous – Jordan of Pisa, Humbert of Romans, Bernardino of Siena, James of the Marches, and Bernardino of Feltre, walked the streets of Europe – and their appearances were heralded days in advance by travellers, street vendors, workers, merchants, and messengers who spoke of their eloquence and the effect they had on the crowds. Often the wait between these advance notices and the appearance of the speakers increased expectations and inspired impatience to hear them. The vehemence with which these preachers lashed out at sins and sinners, the punishments so strikingly, vividly, and colourfully described by them, and the threat of the devil, constantly invoked, sometimes prompted collective repentance and self-abasement among spectators.[4]

Besides the preaching friars whose fiery rhetoric filled church squares – occasionally even the external squares and spaces beyond city walls – with mesmerized spectators, there existed additional tools to disseminate Christian moral principles. These were instructional works, written or translated into the vernacular for the comprehension of the many who would not have understood them had they been written in Latin. These works were compositions of an edifying nature, tracts and short manuals on discipline, intended to instruct, educate, and address specific rules and correct religious practices. They presented believers with a detailed itinerary towards spiritual salvation that began with the customary actions of daily life. The issue of sexual ethics, as it was dealt with by the church, thus emerges not only from works by theologians and experts in canonical law but also from educational tools devised for the use of the ministry, from the literature meant to edify and enlighten, and from the hundreds of sermons given by the most well-attended preachers of the era. The totality of the documentation shows that the attitude espoused by the church was neither static nor exempt from internal contradictions but one which remained fundamentally unified.

The inspiration for this attitude lies in the powerful and tragic story at the start of the book of Genesis, the beginning of everything, when Eve succumbed to temptation. Whether commented upon or interpreted by exegetes in different ways, Eve's actions – the sin committed, the incitement to sin, and the corruption of Adam – forever typify the guilt of all women.[5] God wanted the human species divided into two sexes. However, as suggested by Saint Augustine in his commentary, he did not make them equal. Instead he created woman alongside man as his helper and subordinate and destined the two bodies to fuse in the unity of marriage. The act of marriage, however, does not abolish the inequality or cause us to forgive the original sin: man fell on account of woman and was damned because of his weakness. The body and the spirit, the spiritual element and the carnal element, are governed in humankind by *ratio* (reason), which is said to be *virilis* (of man). Reason is identified with man. The female principle coincides with *appetites* or desire. Even though she is also gifted with reason, instinct – the animal part – prevails in the nature of woman while man is dominated by the rational or spiritual.[6] Upon meditating on Genesis, the Latin fathers of the church, Saint Jerome, Saint Gregory the Great, and Saint Ambrose, agreed that the spiritual side of the human condition was to be recognized in Adam while that of sensuality was to be recognized in Eve. Evil comes from the body and therefore from woman, from the carnal, which is not illuminated by rational spirituality.[7] It is for this reason that man is given the task of controlling feminine impulses, directing their appetites, monitoring behaviours, and punishing if necessary. Due to her weakness and disorderly instincts not held in check by rationality, Eve sinned doubly: against God, by disobeying his will, and against Adam, in trying to dominate him by forcing him to eat the forbidden fruit. From that point on, the destiny of woman is as sinner, temptress, corruptor, and instigator. Hers is a body forever marked by impurity and guilt: it is enticing and seductive but dangerous and deceptive as well.

Thus the church is committed to disciplining sexual behaviour and allowing it only within marriage because the conjugal bond purges the sex act of sin so long as it is "appropriately" (*debito modo*) carried out – with the intention of preserving the human species. According to the Archbishop of Florence, Saint Antoninus, in the mid-fifteenth century: "*Venerea dicuntur actus carnales … In se autem non sunt illiciti, sed quum sunt in ordinati, vide licet contra regula rationis. Unde in conjugio, debito modo servato, absque peccato sunt.*"[8] (It is said that carnal acts are lascivious … [I]n themselves they are not illicit, but only when they are uncontrollable, and go against the rule of reason. Thus, in marriage, performed appropriately, they are without sin.) Concupiscence and pleasure must be subordinate to moderation and to the rule of reason within the marital relationship as well, and in order to distance oneself from any situation that would inspire lust, temptation, and sin, one must eschew idleness, excessive frequentation of women, gluttony, and immoderate imbibing of wine. Thinking about pleasure, dressing and acting lasciviously, dedicating excessive care to one's own body through the use of creams and perfumes, uttering obscenities, or making obscene allusions will foster vice and encourage fornication.

Within this advocacy for restraint and tempered sexuality, the problem of prostitutes and the practice of prostitution entered the deliberations – the discussion on doctrine and the discipline of behaviours – like an explosion, powerfully distressing and disrupting the sensible calm of censorship and prohibition advocated by the church. Medieval canonists could not but disapprove of prostitution and condemn prostitutes, but they should have prevented the problem by pointing the right way forward to civic and legal powers. These women were clearly incurring a serious sin, repeating it over and over again, making it a way of life. They were harming themselves and others to whom they meted out damnation, corroding their most precious resource: the soul. They are hateful, states the Dominican preacher Humbert of Romans in the thirteenth century, and fornication is in itself a vile and shameful sin.[9] To surrender one's own body to so many men – a horrific form of promiscuity – exposes one to the risk of incest, something that would add guilt upon guilt. In the medieval era, the degree of kinship was taken to the fourth order and included acquired relatives, not related by blood, as well as many spiritual relatives, such as godfathers, godmothers, and important elders.[10] And yet, alongside this powerful condemnation was a certain pragmatism put forward by the church, an ambiguity characterized by cynical indifference toward women: prostitution came to be tolerated and justified as *male minore* (the lesser evil). Accordingly, though fornication was a sin and prostitution sinful, better to force some women into prostitution than risk the corruption of virgins, nuns, and honest wives or, worse, have some resort to the "abominable vice of sodomy." The hypocrisy and ambivalence of religious doctrine in this regard led some pragmatic theologians to maintain that prostitutes had a function, a social use, a true *ministerium* (occupation), a term from which is derived the French *métier* and the Italian *mestiere*[11] and in Latin signified a service. Saint Augustine in the *De ordine* and in the *De civitate Dei* very clearly stated the church's reasoning on the subject. Speaking about the weakness of the flesh and the inclination towards libidinous behaviour, and given that one could not persuade nor force another towards continence (unless he were a religious person or in order to avoid something worse such as lust), the church came to tolerate prostitutes and pimps. Just as Moses had permitted the disowning of one's wife by the men of his people in order to avoid murder and after he had found out how widespread the practice had become and that it had been adopted almost as a viable form of separation, so, too, *ecclesia permittit, id est sustinet meretrices et scortatores*[12] (the church permits and tolerates prostitutes and their protectors). Centuries later, in a vernacular that is understandable and effective, Giordano da Pisa (Jordan of Pisa) more or less repeated the same concept:

> God always loathes the greater evils, and from every evil that he tolerates he always retrieves a greater good ... And so an evil is suffered in order to preserve a greater good, and sometimes more than one good. Now do you see the prostitutes of the cities being tolerated? This is a great evil, and if we avoided it, yes, we would be taking away a great benefit, in that there would be more adultery, more sodomy, which would be much worse.[13]

Ivo of Chartres, a bishop and canonist living between 1040 and 1115, in maintaining the indissolubility of the conjugal union and its essentially spiritual nature, believed that it was "worse to profane the marriage of another – that is, commit adultery – than to lie with a prostitute."[14] The Augustinian principles, enlarged upon by the thirteenth century Dominican monk and theologian St Thomas Aquinas in his *Summa* and, above all, in the *De regimine principum*, found application in this Christian message and inspired the behavioural guidelines of the church. The concept of the "lesser evil," useful as a means to avoid much more serious and dangerous evils, had legitimized the tolerance of prostitution for centuries – not of the prostitutes themselves (the sinners and corruptors, those contaminated and rejected) but of the phenomenon – because it allowed men the release of their "licentious passions" and preserved the virtue of respectable women, virgins, and married women so that they might maintain their purity and not offend other men, suitors, or husbands within the sacred bond of marriage. Salvatore Tramontana has written, in a succinct and very effective way, that the Augustinian concept was destined to reduce "man to a woeful mixture of weakness and egotism."[15]

According to the view shared by theologians, men of the church, and preachers, and used actively and advantageously by civil society, it was better to commit women to prostitution, allowing them to exercise the "profession," rather than risk corrupting other honest women. Perhaps more important was the use of prostitution as a guard against the "abominable vice of sodomy," an execrable and scandalous sin against the laws of nature, "against God and His will," "a vice so ugly that it is not appropriate for any wise and gentle soul." "The sodomite of the devil" is what St Bernardino of Siena calls homosexuals when hurling abuse at those who do not obey the will of God who "made woman and man so that they may love each other." The sodomite, "wrapped up in the awful and pernicious sin of cursed sodomy," will end up unleashing divine wrath and "God … do you know what He will do? He will send down upon you war, pestilence, and famine … until there will be no more cattle, no possessions, no gardens, and not even people left."[16]

The great fear was that divine wrath would devastate human life, leaving a desert where once were luxuriant fields and blooming gardens. Deprived of sustenance, humans and animals would die. Plagues, famine, and wars would decimate cities. Corpses would accumulate in the streets. This was both a horrifying imagined scenario and a recurring reality in medieval times when economic crises, conflicts, and epidemics occurred with greater frequency. It is not coincidental then that some of the measures regulating prostitution were adopted from the middle of the fourteenth century, or at the beginning of the fifteenth, in the aftermath of recurring collective tragedies and after the plague had thrown its deadly mantle over Europe, a time when people truly feared that God had abandoned them because of scandals, the relaxing of ethical standards, dissolute licentiousness, and the spreading of the most abhorrent vices: sodomy, adultery, and rape.

Theologians offered a theoretical basis of support for the new municipal laws regulating prostitution, going so far as to defend the legal existence of public brothels (St Vincent Ferrer, who lived from the middle of the fourteenth century to the beginning of the fifteenth, is an example), accept charity from prostitutes, and require a tithe on their earnings by defending the principle of legitimacy with a legal loophole. Their argument was that although the prostitute behaved despicably, the act of prostitution was legal, and therefore a part of her earnings must be allocated for the assistance of others or donated regularly to the church. At the same time, from the thirteenth century onward, the church began its work of conversion and aid towards public women and, in some cases, this took the form of prevention through the financing of dowries for impoverished young women. In order to encourage the reentry of street women and women of the brothel into an honest life of matrimony, Innocent III, in a papal bull of 1198, promised to pardon the sins of those who had taken a repentant prostitute as a wife. In 1227 another pope, Gregory IX, gave the newly formed Order of St Mary Magdalene the right to create houses and refuges for the penitent. This rehabilitation work occurred within a vast penitential movement aimed at saving prostitutes from sin and their clients from constant temptation. By restoring these women to the community, through marriage or by relegating them to separate communities (like the institutions of the converted or of St Magdalene) the church accomplished its goal of limiting the number of prostitutes and of conducting a healing activity. The provision of dowries to girls of marriageable age, too poor to generate the minimum necessary to contract a marriage, enabled the church to save a few women from a destiny that was sometimes inevitable.[17] A decent dowry would attract some young men who due to their own poverty were not able to create a family. A dowry offered the opportunity of a normal life to girls at risk of social downgrading and who might otherwise be dangerously attracted to a world governed by different rules, a world in which they could get lost.

3

A Utopia: The Laws and the Public Authorities

Containing crime and guaranteeing the safety and well-being of citizens was the first priority for the proper functioning of states in the medieval era. Laws and punishments, inquisitions by the Holy Office, and trials and sentences were all part of a system organized to discourage and punish. The system relied on the severity of the prevailing regulations, the efficiency and effectiveness of tribunals and judiciaries, and the ability of governors and armed forces to limit crimes, identify the guilty, and prevent violence and attacks on people and their property. However, through a study of judicial records, trial documents, sentences, appellate proceedings, pardons, and city chronicles, it does not appear that these measures and the widespread deployment of energies succeeded in their intent – neither in terms of eliminating crime nor, in many countries, of containing it. "Dishonest living" characterized the great capitals of Europe – London, Paris, Milan, Venice, Florence, the Spanish and German cities – and also, although to a lesser extent, the smaller urban centres and even the rural towns and villages. Thefts, injuries, assaults, murders, quarrels, exchanges of insults, gambling, and cheating were commonplace and created tensions, worries, and fear in the communities.[1] Again and again, town criers read the bans and new decrees and reiterated the interdiction on carrying arms. This daily ritual was intended in part to teach visiting foreigners about the laws and customs of the city but was also a way for the many citizens who crowded the streets and squares to learn about new regulations and remember old ones. Foreigners, merchants, vendors of all types, shoppers, workers, beggars, passing soldiers, coachmen, servants, and slaves traversed the crowded spaces, met each other, and had occasion to clash. In medieval cities, the participation of so many in addition to those directly involved amplified insignificant incidents that would otherwise have gone unnoticed. Civic leaders had their own armed men in charge of public safety, and these kept an eye out for disorderly conduct as well as real crimes. Records show they were continually preoccupied with "scandals," "noisy commotions," and disturbances or popular uprisings.

Even simple adolescent pastimes frequently had a wild side. In city streets the games commonly played among groups of youths took on aspects of real warfare between opposing sides. The players were mostly salaried workers, still boys, working off excess energy. Alongside their fellow workers they formed "gangs" and engaged in the game popularly called "stone throwing" (*ludum quod vulgariter dicitur la saxaiuola*). These pretend battles sometimes degenerated into bloody and gruesome attacks that ultimately, on occasion, caused injury and death.[2] In the winter of 1426, in Florence, for example, the youth of "higher status" (belonging to the upper classes) had fun tossing stones and rocks at passersby, lapsing into violence once again despite the denunciations of some respectable citizens and the subsequent judicial prohibition of these assaults. The surnames of the culprits showed they came from families of eminent position and explained the arrogance with which they had ignored, on various occasions, the order to immediately cease their behaviour. The Florentine Magistrates of the Eight, aware of their own power and not liking to be ignored, condemned the culprits to a substantial financial penalty in order not to let the crime go unpunished but, above all, so that those responsible could not boast of having defied them.[3] In Barcelona the flinging of stones bore no semblance to a game but was an explicit act of hostility, even among children, often motivated by religious or race hatred that resulted, on more than one occasion, in serious effects.[4]

Although these were minor offences within the broad and differentiated world of crime – which included thefts, injuries, and homicides – in sparsely populated areas even such scandals and incidents had extraordinary repercussions and deeply affected the lives of the individuals by modifying relationships within the community and those between families. It was this tearing of the social fabric, often having unpredictable consequences that included animosity, reprisals, and revenge, that caused considerable worry. Within this context, crimes of a sexual nature acquired distinctive importance. Fornication, rape, sexual assault, and homosexuality – considered deviant – were not considered simple infractions of the law. These transgressions were seen as "vices" and "wrong-doings." They went beyond the limits of the individual and involved public image and collective morality; the entire community might be deemed guilty in the face of divine judgment. Narrative sources offer innumerable examples of how medieval peoples continually turned to the supernatural to explain catastrophic, unusual, and extraordinary events. As they had no great understanding of the natural world, medieval peoples took such catastrophes as the mark of divine and inscrutable intelligence.

The generations who survived the hardships of the mid-fourteenth century – the great blight of the plague and its successive waves that recurred with tragic punctuality, the economic crises, the savagery of wars, and the violence of social uprisings – contemplated the times through which they were living, as well as the future, with discomfort, fear, and mistrust. To understand and accept this great collective tragedy and its consequences in terms of daily life, many attributed the events to the sins that had been committed, ones that had visited upon God an offence so immeasurable as to become forgivable only through the retribution of entire communities. Only by punishing those guilty of crimes, specifically those of lust and unrestrained sexuality (and particularly those against nature) could one placate divine wrath and save humanity from an even more terrible punishment. Only by pursuing those guilty of heinous offences could the "good citizens" be liberated from the vortex of calamity, could wars come to an end, the plague be eliminated, and their enemies thwarted.[5] Representations of debauchery and corruption leading to punishment and divine wrath, which had after all been concretely manifested in the scourges of famine, war, and pestilence, inspired schemes for controlling morality and governing prostitution.

"The wrath of the Almighty will target the sons of men, the nation, and inanimate things with a terrible judgement." These words were spoken on 14 April 1418 and later written down – so as to remain chiselled into memory – not in a religious context but during a sitting of the *Signoria*, the supreme governing body of the city of Florence, and elaborated upon in a document formally produced within the chancellery of the highest political power.[6] The cause of this fearsome and anticipated anger was a wicked vice against nature – the "most nefarious" sin of sodomy – which daily brought new horrors staining the community and preoccupying the governors. Although they were uncertain as to which measures to take, the chancellors were aware of the abyss opening before them, waiting to swallow them up in a wreckage the likes of Sodom and Gomorrah if they didn't act decisively, rapidly, and effectively. Though neither rapid nor effective, their assessment was decisive. Even the Sienese statutes of the early fourteenth century persisted in defining male homosexuality as "horrible, abominable, a most grave sin of perdition of the soul and the body," a definition that was reasserted in the laws of the early fifteenth century.[7]

But other considerations, above and beyond the deplorable events of these decades, impelled authorities in various European countries to take measures to stem the tide of bad behaviour and stop the disorder. These were closely related to societal shifts caused by demographic displacement and the modification of demographic structures resulting from economic and financial problems, worrisome impoverishment, the uprooting of people, fluctuations in manpower and a generalized disturbance in the labour market, and the migration of many young and unmarried men into the cities.

Violence against women intensified, playing a considerable role in increasing the political will to move away from chaos and towards order, harmony, rationality, and efficiency. Research by the historian Jacques Rossiaud into the fifteenth century legal archives of Dijon shows an elevated number of violent crimes against women. Each year about twenty public attacks were reported, verified, and prosecuted, unusual in that, due to shame or fear, rapes were most often hushed up and not reported. Of the cases studied by the French historian, 80 percent were assaults involving more than one attacker, carried out at night by unmasked assailants. Most were attacks on solitary women that involved forcing the victim into a home or abducting her to a secluded place where the assault took place. On these occasions, neighbours were reluctant to intervene, fearing they'd be attacked themselves and not knowing how to challenge a group of delinquents.[8] Most perpetrators were young citizens belonging to the artisan and salaried classes, but there were also episodes involving wealthy and highly placed citizens and foreigners. The victims owed their solitariness to widowhood, the absence of a husband due to work-related reasons, war, and imprisonment, or because they no longer had a family to rely on. In an effort to get help, some of the women resorted to the most feared danger of the time: fire. A fire would have caused the largest number of people to descend into the street, while a cry for help against a rapist would not have solicited attention or brought assistance.

Similar behaviour was recorded in other regions and cities including Venice, Florence, Sicily, Catalonia, Champagne, and Provence. So widespread was this phenomenon that it became a kind of quasi-normality in urban life, to the extent that the search for and punishment of the guilty was limited. This was compounded by the fact that the victims were among the weakest and most defenceless members of society, women who did not belong to the rich families of quality whose doors and defence structures could not be easily broken down. These collective assaults – possibly rituals of masculine initiation – as well as those by individual men, were directed towards unmarried and married women, and widows of humble circumstance. The victims were vulnerable because of the work they did, the unprotected nature of their homes, or the mere fact of walking or travelling in open spaces, often on their own. Some were women of the countryside, attacked while harvesting crops in the absence of a husband, transporting grain to be milled, or young shepherdesses watching over their flocks. Some were enticed by means of trickery while drawing water from the well. Others were surprised at night, and some fell prey to bargemen tasked with ferrying people across rivers. They were easy victims, due to the fragility of their social position and because they were vulnerable and defenceless. They were also convenient victims, chosen because in many locations one paid for one's crime according to one's ability to pay – the sanctions were less substantial for persons of humble circumstance – and the value of a woman's virtue was relative to her status. Imagine an underage, abandoned girl who grew up in a shelter for the vulnerable. One night she is taken by surprise, raped, and then convinced to keep silent. Afterward, she is subjected repeatedly to sexual assaults by a particular young man who is eventually caught and condemned to a pecuniary fine but then released from prison precisely because he is young and poor.[9] Poverty and youthfulness justified the behaviour of a Florentine miller who had committed a series of very serious acts according to the city's laws. First, he had broken the nightly curfew. Then, in the company of a friend, he had attempted to enter a home by pretending to belong to the bodyguard service of the *Podestà* (medieval equivalent of the city state's mayor). He was seeking a girl he had noticed for some time and whom he had chosen as a potential victim. Since no one had answered or opened the door of the first home, the two entered a neighbouring house where they threatened the proprietor and tied him up in an effort to get him to tell them where the girl was. Ultimately they broke down another door in that same house, finding a terrified mother and her young daughters hidden under the bed.[10] In the meantime, the resulting clamour had attracted the attention of others and the perpetrators were caught. The charges were numerous and serious, but in recognition of his youth, poverty, and the fact that he was incapable of supporting himself except by the sweat of his brow, the culprit was released. Poverty and the fact that if incarcerated he'd have been unable to work excused him from the financial penalty. It may also be that the judges justified his audacious behaviour because he was young or that youth offered them the pretext of conferring grace because it was responsible for his violent urge to satisfy an uncontrollable lust.

This case was resolved without grave consequence beyond the fright and humiliation of those whose home the assailants had entered. This was nothing compared to what happened to a Pisan woman, unjustly accused of conducting a scandalous life and of prostituting a girl of ten years whom she was taking care of along with four others. When investigated, following a complaint, she said that through torture and harassment her accusers had induced her to confess to a crime she had not committed. Afterwards it was discovered that her accusers were the same men who one night had knocked at her door and then began to harass her when she refused to open up. Tired of their insistence, the woman opened a window and poured a pail of water over them. This caused them to retaliate by lodging the complaint that resulted in her imprisonment.[11] One can easily see how their different positions were viewed by the law: a sophisticated man, caught in the act of committing a crime, which though not fully executed represented the last in a series of attempts, is pardoned, while a falsely accused woman is subjected to torture so that she confesses to a crime dreamed up out of revenge and supported by false evidence accepted by judges without a thorough investigation. False accusations were not infrequent. They were used to bend women to one's will, subject them to one's desires, or to avenge a rejection. Blackmail and the difficulty for most women to defend themselves were counted on. Judges certainly were aware of the repetition of these deeds and knew that in each case the woman's honour would be stained – thus creating a grey zone, an atmosphere of doubt and suspicion – but it was not for that reason that they felt obliged to act cautiously.

This indulgence with regard to youthfulness, juvenile passions, and the "lascivious" impulses of unmarried men seems to be a constant in the tolerance and exoneration of those who judged and suppressed crime. The fact that other factors – deception, force, threats, and beatings – were often involved did not alter the complicity enveloping the proceedings of the magistrates. At the same time, the opposite was true for the female victims. The women who had been raped, whether married or not, would never be the same afterward. In addition to personal trauma, they would have difficulty reintegrating themselves into their family or social setting. Already most likely in a disadvantaged position, a young girl would be further hindered in obtaining a suitable husband. A married woman would forevermore be singled out by her neighbours and relatives and sometimes abandoned by her spouse. The rapists used scorn, humiliation, offence, and brutality in crushing the will and annihilating the dignity of their victims. Although blameless, the victim would begin to doubt herself, and, although innocent, become the object of scandal. Together with the infamy heaped on her, doubts as to her honesty and questions about her prior behaviour would emerge. She would never recover her honour and would suffer a distancing between herself and others, between herself and "honest" women. When physical violence was perpetrated on a married women it also prejudiced, through a form of adultery, the honour of her husband, and this made the act more serious because it constituted a threat to society.

However, as Jacques de Vitry, the thirteenth-century bishop and cardinal, sermonized, humans are not like animals and are constantly in heat,[12] and lust is a phenomenon that undermines the institution of marriage, destroys families, and erodes the civil order. In agreement, many European legislators between the fourteenth and fifteenth centuries believed they had identified a suitable remedy for these maladies in the form of "municipalized fornication." Prostitutes would mitigate the aggression of young males by satisfying their needs, and this would safeguard the virtue of honourable women. The politics of the governing classes was about reconciling theological and judicial regulations, as well as their medical knowledge of sexuality, with the concrete, such as the daily life couples within the large-scale context of economic and social realities. The demographic and economic growth of the thirteenth century had caused the urbanization of large numbers of young men and poor women from the countryside, all in search of work. The establishment of universities and creation of student collectives (unmarried men) put the orderliness of city life in jeopardy, while the increase of workers in the artisan trades caused a rise in the numbers of men living alone. These factors generated another more specific change: an extraordinary escalation at the end of the thirteenth century in the number of people engaged in the business of prostitution.

Within citizens' councils and governing bodies discussions began to revolve around remedies and provisions that might prevent, or at least control, some of the problems engendered by these changes. Regarding disturbances of a sexual nature, the solution was to create or consolidate urban brothels, considered the best way to allow unmarried men to legally satisfy their sexual instincts. Establishing houses of prostitution would result in the avoidance of much more serious crimes – such as assaults on virgins, married women, honest widows, and nuns – which were on the rise everywhere and worrying municipalities.

Protocols around prostitution and its organization into forms appropriate to urban life represented a constant element in political planning for the control of sexual disturbances and crimes. Favouring, enhancing, legalizing prostitution, and placing it under the management of public authorities also represented an aspiration towards correcting, and possibly eradicating, those behaviours considered "against nature" – homosexuality and sodomy – by encouraging productive unions and marriage. Prostitutes would be the educators of "normal" sexual relations, while redirecting male excesses, violent urges, and the aggressive satisfaction of sexual needs towards moderate and orderly release in places conveniently made available for them. Men, no longer frustrated, needful of infractions or the breaking down of locked doors, no longer permanently tainting women in the name of a masculine rite of initiation, would be tamely reintegrated into the community, the workforce, and the family. In this way, the prostitute became a public benefit and her activity considered a service to the community.

However it was still necessary to define projects that would allow for containment of the phenomenon, simultaneously enabling prostitutes to exercise their profession in a decent way, and give clients convenient access to the benefits. As the Florentine governors put it, in exemplary fashion, in their reforms, it was necessary to set up *loca inhonesta*, "indecent places" where women could decently carry out their work, which was indecent in nature. This Latin term alludes not only to the immorality of behaviour but also to the sordidness of the condition and role. All in all, a "decent indecency" was believed possible by identifying the fundamental characteristic in the decorum, measure, and orderliness of conduct, always in relation to a code of honour. Nonetheless, this "decent indecency" belonged to a base and despicable world. From the middle of the fourteenth century, cities in France, Germany, Italy, and the Iberian Peninsula began to set up public houses of prostitution and to identify the spaces allocated for those houses. The management of this new organization was entrusted either to contractors, who paid substantial sums for the privilege, or municipal officials, who usually performed tasks of a fiscal nature. Only Northern Europe and England, except for London, were immune to these changes.[13]

House of ill repute, brothel, bordello, *domus meretricum* (house of prostitution) are the various names for these structures, designating the residence and place of work of public women. In many places they were called "little castle," with obvious allusion to the walls that enclosed the various houses. In towns where there were no walls, only demarcations of the zone or neighbourhood, new names were conferred on the streets: *Malacucina* (kitchen of ill repute), *Malborghetto* (neighbourhood of ill repute), and street of the *Inferno*. But "enclosed" might – for example, in the fifteenth-century regulations of the city of Ferrara, Italy – allude to a form of isolation and separation that allowed prostitutes, on certain days of the week or at certain hours of the day, to leave the houses in which they had been "assembled" so long as they wore regulated symbols and garments. With these measures, which involved the reorganization of widespread public prostitution and its management into a modern and innovative system, half the governments Europe believed they had finally found a solution to the problem. They deluded themselves into thinking they had put an end to many of the acts of violence that bloodied the streets of their cities, to disorder, the rapes of honest women and innocent virgins, adultery, and even to homosexuality. They also imagined they were hindering the exploitation of public women by diminishing the abuses and aggressions perpetrated on them by their clients, protectors, and brothel keepers while protecting respectable women and defending marriage. The governing classes saw commercialized sex as a sort of therapy for personal malaise and collective discomfort, while also preventing the rise of violence of any kind. Attributing a positive function to prostitution, in accordance with the fathers of the church, served, of course, to restore prevailing values – first of which was heterosexuality – and to reinforce a model of behaviour considered acceptable: sexuality exercised in moderation and within a marriage. In pursuing this pipe dream, the governors did not take into consideration the fact that legalizing, improving, and controlling prostitution, purging it of excesses in oppression and aggression, meant no longer questioning the human, religious, and moral legitimacy of the sale of a human being while reproducing a process of financial exploitation. In short, they were stating, once and for all – and with the blessing of the church and the seal of the state – that there were women who one could buy and use as desired, and men who had the right to do this in exchange for money.

Time would expose the fallacy of this illusion. Nothing, beyond that optimistic beginning, seemed to truly improve. The buying and selling of women, the corruption of young servants and slaves, and the rapes continued and, in the meantime, that "honourably indecent" space revealed its true colours as a troubled and troubling place where the people circulating within it were the lowest of the low, often involved in illicit activities and brawls, leading a precarious existence outside of any rules and regulations. In short, the brothel was a place of pleasure but also a holdall of exploitation, criminality, and misery within the city. It fed bad behaviour, and produced models of violence that would become incompatible with the daily life of the community.

PART TWO

The Reality

4

Clandestine Women and Public Women

All the meticulous work of legalization engineered by the municipalities, between the end of the fourteenth century and the first decades of the fifteenth, envisaged public brothels as the mainstay of a plan for the reorganization of laws regarding prostitution, with rules that would discipline life within the walls of the brothel, and would include frequent checks on the part of the authorities monitoring compliance. After careful evaluation by political-administrative bodies, city zones were selected and buildings constructed or adapted with the expectation that fiscal revenues from the activities to take place within them would cover the costs. All officially recognized public women would be enclosed within those boundaries and prohibited from selling their bodies elsewhere. The scandals would finally come to an end. Streets, squares, markets, taverns, and public baths would be free of the awkward presence of flagrantly dressed, loud, and coarse women fighting over a potential client, laughing, soliciting, showing off their personal charms, and generally causing grave concern to decent citizens, especially virtuous women. In Montpellier, residents complained constantly to municipal authorities and royal functionaries that prostitutes and pimps had transformed their city into one big bordello and asked for their banishment. They also protested that such disruptions caused brawls and crimes almost every single day.[1] For quite some time, the growing number of prostitutes had been arousing general disapproval; the new provisions elicited a sense of relief.

Undoubtedly, to the prostitutes, the areas in which they were to be confined, seemed, as in truth they were, houses of segregation, and they did not share the same sentiment as to the new measures nor the general sense of satisfaction. It was one thing to live a life of relative freedom, though often difficult and bitter, on the streets, in the chaotic warmth of the tavern, and the public baths in relative freedom and another to be officially declared a public woman at whom everyone pointed, ripped from her own home, and forced to enter a brothel. Relative freedom because the harlot is never completely free: she is "looked after" by a protector and burdened with debt, dependent on the mood of the tavern proprietors, innkeepers, and the custodians of the public baths and at the mercy of the desires and demands of her clients. It was much better if she could maintain herself, be independent and "clandestine," discreetly and moderately receiving clients in her own home.

Before the authorities held these women in their grasp and before the institution of the brothel, prostitution took diverse forms and was spread throughout the city, countryside, and villages. "Wandering" prostitutes went from hamlet to hamlet, stopped in small rural settlements, and at times associated with shady characters, fraudsters, gamblers, and stray soldiers. They immersed themselves in an ebb and flow of vagrants, outcasts, labourers in search of work, young apprentices, and thieves on the run because of being charged or simply because it seemed the wise thing to do.[2] These were all people passing through and leaving few traces: the occasional record of toll charges or an appearance in the lists of foreigners kept by the guards at city gates or in the notes compiled by hospital rectors taking account of the charity and hospitality provided by the hospices. Prostitutes followed marching armies, moved from festival to festival, and from market to market. The Tuscan mayors of Figline, San Casciano, and Montevarchi repeatedly prohibited the prostitutes from leaving the street assigned to them in each locality but gave up when faced with the evidence that on market day the place was "full of whores shamelessly and scandalously going about and committing every indecent act and word."[3] Sometimes the women stopped over for a while, until ready to take up their wanderings and get back on the road before arousing too much attention from the community. Inns and taverns were open to them and their activities.

These taverns, condemned by the church as places that accommodated drunkenness, prostitution, gambling, swearing, idleness, vagrancy, aggression, brawling, and even murder, were under the supervision of authorities that controlled their hours of operation and unfailingly considered them hotbeds of chaos and the meeting places of uprooted individuals who lived by means of criminal activity. It was here that malcontents gathered, unrest was unleashed, and dangerous sympathies created, not only because of reasons put forward by the clergy but also because ideas of dissent circulated within the tavern's walls. The "commoners," the workers who mainly frequented these places, used the occasion of a drink, and often more than one drink, to broadcast and comment upon the news, to complain of their fatigue, harsh work conditions, and low wages. The feeling of impotence, individual frustration, and injustice thus concentrated there and contributed to the formation of opinions and ideas, and sometimes developed into collective demands. More than anything else, the powers-that-be feared agitation, turmoil, upheaval, or the unexpected flare-up of rebellion; for this reason, too, they looked suspiciously upon those places with the worst reputation, where groups of troubling, worrisome, and dangerous people, made up of passing soldiers, professional hustlers, pickpockets, and con artists, represented a constant threat. A large clientele of customary but feared regulars for these establishments came from the communities of foreigners residing in medieval cities. Excessive in their drinking habits, they easily got drunk and severely irritated. Furthermore, they carried weapons, although those were prohibited, thus endangering the safety of other patrons. On an evening in March 1426, the German, Giovanni di Gherardo, imbibed a good number of drinks in one of the many Florentine taverns, and, under the effect of so much wine, had lost control of himself. Not considering the danger, he unsheathed his sword, despite the prohibition against carrying weapons, and careless as to the consequences began swinging it about. The chief magistrate with his officers disarmed and arrested him, but the prevailing opinion was that it was the habit of foreigners to always drink too much, inevitably ending up inebriated.[4] Merchants, travellers, and foreigners in transit were forced to use the services of the taverns though they were well aware of the risks and dangers encountered within them. They were worried about choosing the best of them – those with a good reputation – but that did not necessarily protect them from dangerous encounters and unfortunate incidents. Within this milieu, prostitutes were, along with the wine and food, an attractive feature, and tavern proprietors often designated certain rooms for their use. These were sometimes above the large common room, in a nearby hotel, or in "huts," "cabins," or "small cottages" in the area and were rented to the prostitutes or their pimps.

Since the twelfth century, public baths, also called *stufe* (saunas) and sometimes *terme* (thermal baths), were widespread in Europe. They existed in France, Flanders, Germany, Italy, and Spain, and were not confined to large cities (Paris, Bruges, Basil, Venice, and Florence) but existed also in minor centres like Avignon, Chartres, and Dijon.[5] These baths came into being for legitimate reasons and safeguarded reputations with harsh regulations and the presence of caretakers who ensured that men and women used the baths on alternate days or at different times and guarded against, or were supposed to, illicit behaviour. Despite that, the baths ended up becoming pleasure centres where men were offered services by obliging women who were on the premises precisely to "serve" them, offer every care in the bath, massage and, ultimately, satisfy them sexually. All of this was forbidden, and city magistrates did what they could to prohibit these activities and reaffirm the laws, but inspections were often superficial and lax, not to mention frequently complicit. A choicer clientele – compared to the taverns – frequented the baths. Many of the men were married and had important positions within their communities. One could even find members of the clergy there. All in all, this meant that prudence in supervision and in making complaints seemed almost obligatory. Machinations intended to elude regulations and surveillance abounded and were well designed: hospitality would be given to couples, providing the appearance of legitimacy, who claimed the inability to find lodging in a suitable hotel. Concealed secondary doors could be opened to them. Sometimes male clients pretended to have involuntarily fallen asleep, thus remaining inside during the hours reserved for female clients. We can easily understand how the Sienese statutes could claim that "in the public baths horrible and mortal sins are committed"[6] and why the Florentine governors took provisions against prostitutes, pimps, and "depraved individuals" who disgraced the neighbourhood and the entire city by coming and going at their convenience from the Terme di San Michele Berteldi by way of a secret door that the proprietors of the baths had already been ordered more than once to wall over.[7] Moreover, this last charge came towards the end of the fifteenth century when the system of regulated prostitution inside brothels had been established and consolidated for decades.

If corruption in the public baths had become a widespread reality and seemed to be irrefutable and not surprising to anyone – neither to the authorities nor the clients or God fearing citizens, and certainly not to nearby residents – what does surprise is that we can trace a scandalous situation to the oldest, most prestigious, esteemed, and famous hospital in Florence, the Hospital of Santa Maria Nuova. In a passionate letter to Lorenzo the Magnificent, a hospital assistant, Caterina Muccingrifi, complained of corruption and serious scandal within the institution, where people gambled, prostitutes turned up, and sodomy was rapidly spreading, all with the complicity of a priest named Antonio and the tacit collusion of the hospital's administrator. Obviously the woman had no faith in the hospital rector or other persons in charge of the administration of Santa Maria Nuova and so turned directly to Lorenzo de' Medici in an attempt to reach someone who might not be complicit or corruptible at the apex of power. In her words we have a merciless accusation of the most serious of activities, harmful to the respectability of the institution, its proper functioning, and the decency and dignity of those responsible.

> In days gone by, in going to the Hospital as was my wont, I discovered a public prostitute at the head of a table, eating with other women. I asked who she was. I was told that she was the whore of Father Antonio and that it was necessary to treat her with honour in order to keep the peace with him … and I went, protective of the honour of the place, and said so to Messer Andrea, believing that he would want to see to this, as it was within his purview. He answered me that it was necessary to bear with this and other things and that nothing could be done against him. I said to him that if he did not take care to throw that whore out of the hospital and remove the gambling that went on every day, as well as the acts of sodomy that were being performed there, it would be a serious reason for all of the women presently in the hospital to leave.

Initially, Caterina attempted to make an internal complaint, for which she received only the hatred of Father Antonio and his immediate revenge. In fact, not two days had passed when she was thrown out of the hospital "like some wicked woman." This is how her passionate pleas came into being: "for which, Lorenzo the Magnificent, I and the other poor women appeal to Your magnificence … so that this merciful place will not be a gambling den and a bordello for men and women."[8] Besides the question of scandal, which is unusual to find in the form of an accusation and, moreover, addressed to the highest authority in Florence, what is striking is her sense of the institution's honour and her awareness of its mission "of mercy," both of which had been altered by the corruption and complicity.

The above mentioned forms of prostitution cannot be defined as clandestine and private. These women solicited clients in public, on the streets, in the market squares, in locations crowded with men, in the ports, and mills, and, as we have seen, even in a hospital. Their intentions were unequivocally recognizable, if not conspicuously labelled. However, these women were not yet subject to the constraints of the brothel, its internal regulations and to restrictions on their movement, and, as far as being recognizable, they could try to disguise themselves, avoiding observation when they wished. In being a secret prostitute, *encubierta* as she would have been called in Spain, a woman had to possess the will to operate outside of any structure – hotels, taverns, and baths of ambiguous reputation. The clandestine prostitute received men in her own home or found another private house in which to conduct her business and where she might have associated with other prostitutes with whom to share expenses, rooms, and sometimes clients. Often the women, accused of immorality and scandalous conduct, were widows. For example, in Troyes, four or five widows got together and received clients in their house – their affairs were well known to everyone – until they were accused of behaving like public prostitutes.[9] Frequently foreign women found themselves in this situation: having lost their husbands, possibly the only source of income for the family, and having been uprooted from their country of origin, they were without sufficient support or the ability to otherwise earn a living. Sometimes a mother and her daughter or daughters were forced into the same circumstances as "indecent" women "who offered up their body to lust as prostitutes" and blatantly engaged in "lustful and wicked vices."[10] Other times it was married women who had the support and complicity of their husbands, or humble artisans who thought about integrating incomes, keeping two or three women, who prostituted themselves, and for whom they directly procured clients. Perhaps these women were even prostitutes who had left the public brothel and were trying to redevelop a clandestine business.

This represented the best possible situation: one without ties to protectors and brothel keepers and, with few exceptions, no restrictions or the infamy of being registered as a public prostitute. These women were free to conduct a normal life, to go out, travel anywhere, and meet "good citizens" and "respectable women" without being rejected. These hidden lives, however, did not last long and almost always ended up being widely known, leaving the women disgraced by a bad reputation.

"Do not ever go to the home of any worldly woman, or someone similar, at night," recommended Paolo da Certaldo, "if for some reason she might send for you, and if she sends for you many times, tell her to come to your house, if she wishes to come; if not, and if one remains, know that many terrible things have been seen, especially in lands by the sea and foreign lands."[11]

In treatises on behaviour, advice such as that of Paolo da Certaldo was not infrequent, and in literature, the nasty misadventures that befell merchants and foreigners in the homes of women of easy virtue were often the entertaining central point of the plot in many stories by famous storytellers from Sacchetti to Boccaccio and Masuccio Salernitano to Sercambi.

Although prudence and various precautions were adopted, the comings and goings of men from these widely known houses at every hour of the day, and now and then even at night, soon became obvious. It happened that youth and adolescents, perhaps less inclined to discretion and controlled behaviour, gathered in front of the doors of prostitutes' dwellings. Medieval houses, moreover, did not enjoy a large amount of privacy. With dwellings ranging from the bourgeois palace to the hovel of the most humble labourer attached to each other, sometimes with small communal courtyards and walls that enabled one to hear what was happening on either side, neighbourhoods provided for a well-informed public, keenly aware of nearby brazen behaviour, and the whisperings eventually developed into voices of contempt and disapproval. God-fearing and respectable persons of a more elevated social standing were outraged by the scandals and feared the impact on the honour of their homes and families. Decent, virtuous women who were alone began to fear for their lives and worried about their safety. Old grudges, unresolved quarrels, malicious words uttered in a moment of anger, intolerances generated by proximity, envy, and rivalry, when added together and endured for a long time, would finally explode and prompt acts of vengefulness, bringing about accusations of immorality and scandalous behaviours.

"Bonicives et honeste mulieres" (Good citizens and honest women) signalled the presence of "femene di mala vita, conditione et fama" (women of ill repute, condition, and character) who had made a bordello of where they lived, selling themselves for money and welcoming people of all sorts and of poor character: thieves, charlatans, whores, and pimps. They also pointed to more serious crimes, like the prostitution of girls at a tender age, the offer of young boys to well-known sodomites, abortions, and even infanticide. Determined neighbours once reported having seen a baby of eight or ten days thrown into a well and left there to rot.[12] Most often the accusations had a basis in truth. The medieval clergy were generally harsh when interrogating and deplored false charges, interpreted as an offence to their function and their person, because they had been assigned a public responsibility. Thus they were not lenient in the punishment of false accusers. It also happened that an accusation might have been a total fabrication hiding the intention to unjustly damage an innocent woman. Once the punishment was decreed, however, whether banishment from the city, a fine, or a flogging, trying to prove one's innocence and noninvolvement in the facts as charged became practically impossible. A review and a pardon took a great deal of time and required someone trusted and diligent to follow the procedures and accompany the woman throughout the course of events.

A woman who had behaved as a prostitute in her own home and was then discovered and punished, and perhaps expelled from the territory for a few years, was, nevertheless, capable of maintaining her standing as an infamous but independent woman. The fate was different for those flagged and judged as public prostitutes. They were led away to the brothels and there began a new existence and an activity they had not chosen. Selling one's own body "in secret," even if the term was totally misleading since the fact was well-known, allowed some glimmer of freedom as well as the autonomous management of personal time, men, and practices. And it also allowed for the state of affairs, at times dictated by the necessity of the moment, to be reversed in some way. Reversing one's journey and being restored to a normal life was an aspiration, and it seemed feasible. But being branded by the authorities as a public woman and subjected to the obligations, restrictions, and life circumstances imposed, crushed once and for all that fragile aspiration, nourished by a slim and irrational hope.

But, before becoming a public woman, how did one enter the world of prostitution and arrive at the point where one began to sell one's body to a variety of men? What experiences and circumstances propelled a woman in that direction? Unfortunately, rarely have traces of a woman's journey towards entering this world been preserved. Stripped of their identity, origins, and family belonging, these women become mere shadows that only fleetingly come to life. What we have of them is a name and a place of birth, sometimes not even a name, but a nickname, a designation that refers to a geographic origin or a personal characteristic, often also distorted – a whimsical name perhaps connected to an episode in life unknown to us. All this creates more imprecision and uncertainty around the identification and reconstruction of a woman's trajectory. Poverty and isolation first come to mind as a starting point and motivation, but in order to move on from these valid, yet generic and unnuanced circumstances, it is necessary to resort to interpretations that proceed from concrete and documented evidence. It is possible to hypothesize a commonality, when considering the fate of these women: that of some violence suffered, not so much and not only a physical violence, but one brought to bear on their freedom of behaviour, on their potential to make choices.

Domestic service constituted a first stage. Elisabeth Pavan[13] ascertained this to have happened in Venice. The young girls, seduced and forced to satisfy the desires of their master, sometimes impregnated by the men of the household as well as punished and cast out, perhaps out of retaliation at the request of offended wives, ended up continuing on a path they had not chosen and which would drive them further and further away from the community. What is more, female servants represented one of the largest groups of young women assaulted and raped by nonmembers of the family for whom they worked. Victims of sexual violence almost never found viable alternatives to the vortex of prostitution into which they had been thrust.

Costanza was a young girl who arrived in Florence from the countryside of the Mugello region in order to work as a domestic. On Berlingaccio day (the Thursday before Lent), a time of playfulness, revelry, good cheer, and fun, she was "assaulted, violated, and sodomized" by "many brutes, who shared her amongst themselves."[14] As a direct result of the gang rape, her employment as a servant was terminated the Fat Thursday during Carnival. Costanza ended up at the "Buco," one of the many infamous taverns of the city. Slaves were treated differently even if designated for domestic service and subjugated to the desires of the men of the family. They could not abandon the house in which they lived: they belonged to the master. They were a part of his estate, like movable assets, and thus completely under his control. And no one could take them away without having to undergo the inevitable penal consequences, nor could slavewomen find refuge in a brothel, even if they wanted it, without running the risk of being quickly brought back and punished.

The laws – continuously adapted, improved, and broadcast – seemed to function very poorly. Penalties were imposed, for instance, on "he who might lead astray the servant or slave of another. And on whomsoever keeps and conceals her, and on who enters into the home of another in order to take advantage of such a slave or servant and on he who impregnates her," but when it came to punishing the "corruptors and seducers of the said young girls," the law's lack of clarity was invoked. The guilty argued that it was not clear whether the law referred only to slaves or also to servants, who were free, even though they were working in the home of another – a specious argument since the text of the regulation was actually absolutely clear cut and unequivocal. Nonetheless the guilty were not punished, and every day their audacity in perpetuating these offences increased.[15]

Debts and extreme poverty were at the root of many individual stories. When wives were abandoned or separated from a husband for various reasons – a quest for work that took him far away, a betrayal, some impediment beyond their control such as a legal sentence, or being captured in war – they were often incapable of finding respectable work and so had to resort to the expedient of selling their bodies as a quick and immediate solution to the problem of survival without believing entirely that they would become so enmeshed in that new life as to ultimately lose sight of an alternative. This was in part because they acquired the indelible stain of a bad reputation and in part because they became prey to exploiters. And then there were those girls, deluded and deceived by false promises of marriage by young men or professional seducers who merely craved a sexual relationship, as well as young women who became pregnant due to an extra-marital relationship, and those who were raped. Of course the solution of prostituting oneself was not taken for granted by everyone, but it certainly was the most probable. This was so because if, on the one hand, there was the urgent necessity of earning a living in order to survive, on the other hand, prostitution represented a complete removal of the traditional cornerstones of existence. Social tenets of behaviour were so strict that they seldom allowed for tolerance and most often called for the expulsion of the woman from society. Thus there was an added condemnation and censure upon the woman, as well as the impossibility of insertion or reinsertion into the community. Besides, many of these women, dishonoured even if innocent, became the object of scandal in the eyes of their neighbours, sometimes of their lovers, and even in their own eyes because the general attitude prompted them to perceive themselves as no different than prostitutes.

A microcosm revolved around these single women or around women of poor families, widows, or unhappily married women who, by means of flattery, threats, or promises, could be robbed of their lives. The people within this microcosm were criminals who intended to live off these women, elder procuresses, young wage earners or wastrels, recruiters of prostitutes, professional seducers, and "gluttons of ribaldry." This latter definition, which we find in some manuscripts from the period, expresses most eloquently the gluttonous and greedy desire to exploit. Even Bernardino of Siena uses the word "glutton" in one of his sermons. He is referring, however, to the old madams, to those "abhorrent Christians" who, no longer able to sell their own flesh, get by with "selling that of others." Pretending they wish to buy some cloth woven by young widows, the madams insinuate themselves into their homes and with their murmurs and sighs, instil, drop by drop, the poison of corruption: "filia mea, heu quam magnum peccatum tu facis, perdendo ita frustra tuum tempus … quia in veritate tu es pulchrior juvenis istius terrae."[16] ("O my daughter, what a great sin you commit in vainly wasting your time … since, in truth, you are the most beautiful young woman on this earth.") The reference to youth and wasted beauty constituted a powerful enticement to an existence spent amongst deprivations and humiliations. The same work of soliciting on the part of these "drunken and gluttonous" women was brought to bear on poor girls. Bernardino of Siena also said, "She has in mind the desire to fatten up by using your flesh."[17]

A great deal of people had a similar intention "in mind." Among them, we sometimes find the same prostitutes with regard to the daughters they birthed and allowed to survive. The very young, ten to twelve-year-olds, represented a valued commodity in sexual commerce and one that allowed for the earning of good profit. The female children, growing up in this setting of ill repute, were thus launched into the same activity that had spawned them. But it wasn't necessary to be a mother in order to procure a girl to keep in one's grasp in the brothel while she performed some service, including that of training in the art and then being sold.[18] On 14 June 1449, in Rome, for instance, Giuliano di Angelo of Vitorchiano, a resident of the city, was handed a harsh judgment consisting of a fine of fifty ducats, a flogging in the city streets, and the branding on his forehead of the letter L standing for *lenone*, or pimp. He had been prostituting his young daughter for over a year, accompanying her to the homes of clients where she was left for a day and a night, and ultimately making her available in the public prostitution lists.[19] Sexual abuses of minors represented a painful and widespread reality, often concealing an actual initiation into prostitution within a family setting, as we have seen. We have daughters sold by fathers and others exploited by their own mothers. In 1458 Gisellina from Pavia, no more than a child, was raped, and infected with scabies by a circle of merciless adults including her mother, a complicit neighbour (the broker and procuress), and the rapist who had dragged and kicked her into a bedroom and there penetrated her more than once with great difficulty; before the judge and in an attempt to escape the death penalty, the rapist declared Gisellina to be a common prostitute.[20]

A woman could be bought, sold, exchanged, and sent from one town or city to another, exactly like any piece of merchandise. Next to the widespread recruitment into the ranks of public women there existed an adjacent market of greater size. Traffickers in women traded in young women from foreign and distant lands, mainly from the East, perfecting their business movements with fake contracts that provided for the restitution of money used for expenses in travelling, food, clothes, and the fee for engaging them – a practice that has been transmitted down to our time. It was in this way that a woman worked without a salary and without ever glimpsing the possibility of settling her debt, which grew, depending on the whims and the will of the traders, until she lost all personal freedom, being sold, as she was, like a slave, or as a prostitute in yet another country different from the one she arrived in.[21] In any case, public women, once declared as such and sent to work in the brothels, represented an itinerant slice of humanity. It was difficult to settle down for a very long time in the same place, barring a few rare exceptions. Once the rules of engagement were satisfied with their keeper and their debts paid off, they transferred to brothels in other cities and other countries. They remained strangers, outsiders, and foreigners in each and every place.

Poverty, violence, and bondage are not the only common denominators explaining the entry to a journey into prostitution. A single woman could choose to give up her body for compensation and a better wage, for a type of work she considered to be less laborious in comparison to other heavier and less well-paid work that the medieval world provided, for instance, in textile manufacturing, glass production, in the dockyards where ships were built and sails were sewn, in building sites, in excavation work, in houses as domestic servants, as washerwomen, or in the mills and in the bakeries.[22] Sexual services, especially if well paid and outside of the recognized structures, must have sometimes seemed preferable to young women who thought about acquiring money, satisfactions, and a less miserable standard of life with less exertion than the work of manual labourers. Promiscuity, the association with so many men, the enslavement to their desires and wishes, and the prolonged exploitation of their bodies were not thought of as obstacles, neither in a moral sense nor, relatively speaking, in terms of their personal dignity.

5

The Identification of a Public Woman

In order to declare a woman immoral and launch a trial that would define her as a public prostitute, with the inevitable consequences of wearing the symbols dictated by the community in which she lived, or going to live and work in the brothels, it was essential to produce trustworthy witnesses. In Italian cities the number of witnesses required varied, but generally speaking one was expected to provide a minimum of four, as in Florence, or five, as in Siena. Whatever the number was, what counted was not the way in which they came to know about the events in question and the validity of the evidence but, rather, the good reputation that they enjoyed. As for the accusations, promiscuity with men other than her husband, if married, had to be proved. By explicit definition of canon law, a woman available to the desire of many men must be defined as a prostitute, since the essence of the activity is indeed one of promiscuity.[1] However, it was necessary to agree upon the meaning of the concept of promiscuity because civic laws were not always the same. In Cremona, for instance, the law stated that one had to have been with at least four men before being considered a prostitute, whereas in Ferrara if a wife was carnally intimate with anyone other than her husband she had to enter into a brothel.

In Florence, at the start of the fifteenth century, trials of this sort took place quite frequently. They were part of a political will to control private initiative and monitor behavioural discipline. Witnesses against the accused acted mostly as interpreters of public opinion and collective discontent. They constituted an intermediary between the subject under investigation and the neighbourhood, giving voice to the "public notoriety" of the accused, and for that reason were not required to have direct experience of the event. On 5 May 1402, for example, Dame Agnola, resident of the Santa Felicità neighbourhood, was accused of scandalous behaviour and prostitution, without a shadow of doubt, and with great shame experienced by her neighbours. The first witness stated that all respectable people living around the woman knew that she was prostituting herself, and, more specifically, he knew about this because Dame Lucia, a maker of lasagne, and the baker Giovanni had told him. The second witness gave a similar deposition, reporting that there were two priests among the good citizens with whom he had discussed the woman's behaviour. Three more witnesses spoke along the same lines. Only one, a shoemaker, added that she had already been thrown out of the house in which she previously lived for bad conduct.[2] Despite the fact that all those called to testify reported only opinion and gossip and could not personally verify Agnola's scandalous behaviour, she was officially declared a public prostitute. This was part and parcel of judiciary practice and so it should not surprise anyone. However, it represents a useful element toward understanding some mechanisms and reactions. Regularly patronizing a house for the purpose of a paid sexual liaison with the proprietress did not go unnoticed for long: unusual comings and goings of men caused neighbours to comment upon the situation and exchange information. The proprietors of workshops in the area had a privileged vantage point. They knew their own clients and recognized the arrival of strangers in the district. The same could be said of the residents in neighbouring houses. They were the first to see and hear, but condemnation did not take place immediately. Often a long time passed during which the clergy and the most important heads of households were consulted. Only later, when impatience had reached its limit and with concern for the safety of wives and daughters, was the initiative taken to present a case in a public trial.

In proceedings conducted against Selvaggia, wife of a certain Seze, the witnesses were many and proved to be well informed and explicit. The accused, when summoned, presented herself before the court of the illustrious and respectable doctor of law, Giovanni of Montepulciano, judge of the appellate court, and an Official of the *Grascia* Commission (the Office of Meats and Fish) of the city of Florence, but since, according to the statutes, women were forbidden to enter into the domain where a judge was presiding, the notary of the office was commissioned to go to her and, standing on the steps of the entrance, speak to the accused Selvaggia and ask what she had to say on her own behalf. She claimed she was innocent. She was then reminded that she had eight days to prepare her defence. In the meantime, the judge would hear the witnesses, who presented themselves five days after the notice to the accused and, having taken the oath, began to give their version of events.

The first, Antonio di Ugo, a resident of the same area, claimed that he had seen many men enter the woman's house, both citizens and foreigners, night and day, to have seen them larking about with her, strolling with her, and engaging in immoral acts, such as touching and groping her as was usual in behaviour with a prostitute. He had recognized among them some fellow citizens: a barman in a wineshop, a *pianellaio* (a maker of slippers), and many others whose names he did not know. As to reputation and rumour, he reported that almost everyone in the neighbourhood spoke of her as a public prostitute. He was asked to describe her for certainty of identification, and he said that she was tall, quite pretty, brown haired, and around forty-five years of age. The second witness, Vanni di Migliore, confirmed the same accusations: the presence, night and day, of many men, the joking, the going about in an immoral fashion, the bad reputation. He added, however, a specific incident. One night he became aware that her door had been closed from the outside, and he pointed to the slipper maker as the responsible party, someone who was a regular visitor to the Selvaggia household. He had turned to the man to reproach him and told him that he was doing wrong in behaving in this way, and the man in question had answered, "And I will screw whom I please" while Selvaggia herself uttered profanities at him. It is unnecessary to point out that the proximity of the houses impeded any sort of privacy and that curiosity and the desire to observe the goings-on caused neighbours not only to peek out from windows but to keep doors open in order to see better.

With a few slight but important differences, the female witnesses did not diverge much from the men's versions. Paola, after having corroborated the basic ideas already expressed, added that one day, when standing at the threshold of her house, she saw a stranger heading directly to the home of Selvaggia. The man, embarrassed, said to her: "Vos faceretis mellius ad intrandum domum vestram" ("You would do better to go back into your own house"), thus directly corroborating the immoral acts being performed between the walls of the house next door. Margherita was even more explicit: via a window in the house of the accused, she had seen Selvaggia in bed, naked, together with naked men, who were taking their immoral pleasure with her, just as with any common public prostitute.

After having listened to the witnesses and hearing from the defendant, whose testimony was not reported – as if it were irrelevant, of little weight and value – the judged pronounced sentence, which above all pertained to the verification of guilt, namely the fact that Selvaggia "eius corpus prestitit libidini pro lucro pecuniario" ("granted her body in lust for pecuniary gain"). As a consequence, from that moment on, the woman was to be considered and treated as a prostitute, could not go about the streets of the city without wearing the appropriate symbols of her status as such, and would be subjected to all prohibitions dictated for the classification of a public woman.[3]

As has been said, the "bad reputation" of a woman of easy virtue and her associated business activity were often known to her watchful neighbours, who were disposed to endure the goings-on, although complaining of it amongst themselves, with perhaps a mild rebuke, devoid of effect. They were generally inclined towards silence, possibly because they did not want the nuisance of making a complaint or the necessity of having to face a tribunal and the law, which instilled fear and a sense of diffidence, or because they were actually tolerant to some extent or possibly because they did not want to risk disputes and maybe retribution. Then some event, some new development, a bad word, or a slight raised the tension and the scandal exploded, exposing a situation that had existed for years. One must not forget that, according to the laws of some states, it was strictly prohibited to maintain a brothel in one's own house, the penalty for which involved the complete destruction of that house, an occurrence that could, after all, negatively impact the surrounding homes.

In the case of Violante de Fox, from Zaragoza, the lawful wife of Loys Carnier, her being accused and tried for adultery and prostitution was based on the fact that she met with a Jew and retained him as a customer. It was 1474, and it was said that it was the "truth, commonly circulated rumour, belief, opinion, and public repute" that the woman behaved like a prostitute, that she had a good number of clients, whom she entertained for payment, and that her husband was complicit. Seven men and three women, all neighbours, gave testimony against her. Some of them claimed, beyond a shadow of a doubt, to have clearly seen from the window that she entertained her clients while in her house and in the bed *of her husband*. And this specification sounds like an aggravating factor, almost as if it were not about the marriage bed, which is shared. Furthermore, a witness declared that he had seen her lying with the Jew and at the same time with her lawful husband. Condemned "por las puterias e desonestadas" ("for prostitution and immorality"), Violante asserted that she did it because her husband did not provide for her as munificently and as lavishly as her customers.[4]

The issue of money, even beyond that of need and poverty, is important for an understanding of some biographies of clandestine prostitutes. Not being subjugated to any sort of monitoring or limitation, and working in private homes and not in dwellings filled with a great deal of people, the women were able to choose a more select clientele, often including regular visitors, who established a good rapport with them. They were also able to earn a decent living by selling their bodies. The price to pay for all this was the disapproval of their neighbours, who were in the know, the contempt of some of these, and a relative social marginalization within the microcosm of their surroundings. But those among them who did not prostitute themselves only to survive but had chosen and not been forced to do it, developed attitudes of indifference with regard to the opinion of others and of the community. At times, their nonchalance gave rise to an attitude of challenge and aggression. The only risk in this conduct that could perhaps cause anxiety and worry was the complaint of immorality. If the persistence and perseverance in their behaviour and in their attitude of brazenness led to trials, they knew all too well that they had no chance of defending themselves and that the brothel, the bans, the record of being a public prostitute would draw threateningly closer. Prohibitions and symbols would end up putting their stamp upon an existence so different from the one they had been leading, which, even if it was not yet that of the brothels, meant being known, fingered, avoided, often taunted, insulted, and attacked, without judicial protection. In some countries, for example, in view of her status as a "depraved woman" and the fact that she offered up her body to one and all in exchange for money, assaulting a public prostitute was not considered a crime nor was kidnapping her for the purpose of satisfying sexual desire.

6

The Signs of Inequality

In medieval societies, social class, roles, and affiliations were well defined, and the identification of these, through prohibitions, rules, clothes, signs, and symbols, represented a necessity and a value. Distinguishing with instant accuracy the poor man from the rich man, the religious person from the layperson, the Catholic from the Jew, the soldier from the civilian, the doctor from the barber, the magistrate from the common man, the plague victim from the healthy person, the leper from a noncontaminated person, the moral woman from the immoral woman, the public prostitute from all the others, entailed a series of interdictions and obligations. If it is obvious why a layperson was prohibited from wearing priestly garb and the average citizen from wearing the red cloak of a doctor or the uniform of a soldier much less the attire of a judge while exercising his duties – the purpose of such restrictions being to prevent someone from usurping a position and a role they were not entitled to or using a disguise for some illicit goal – the regulations regarding at least four categories were quite different: plague victims, lepers, Jews, and prostitutes. This was partly because it was not just a case of forbidding specific attire but also of imposing a distinctive marking. In many cases, in addition to the rules about clothing and ornamentation, there also existed interdictions against inhabiting certain areas and walking certain streets. Those who fell sick during a plague epidemic were forced into quarantine, segregated within their houses, which were marked with a sign. Their family members and those who had come into contact with them, if allowed to exit their homes, wore a yellow band. Lepers were confined within a *lazzaretto*, or leper hospital, outside the city and entered the circle of city walls only on specific days and hours, carrying with them a bell, which they rang to warn passersby and to keep them far away from any contact and sight. Jews lived in specific communities, in reserved spaces, and wore a label of some kind, usually a round yellow badge on their clothes. In Bologna, however, it was a symbol of a red dog's tongue.[1] Caution is necessary in judging these symbols as acts of violence because undoubtedly they must be incorporated into an understanding of medieval cultural environment and sensibility, that era's need for "codes of distinction." How can we forget, however, that such codes served also to identify individuals and groups on whom violence and subjugation were often inflicted and marked people whose presence had to be made evident in order to avoid contact with them or to simply avoid any kind of ambiguity?

Public prostitutes in the thirteenth and fourteenth centuries were subject to restrictions and obligations in terms of their attire or the places that they could or could not frequent. This situation changed slightly in the fifteenth century with the establishment, almost throughout Europe, of organized prostitution that included reserved spaces and brothels, but bans and badges did not disappear altogether. Specific legislation and different judiciaries also persisted for this category of person. From the second half of the thirteenth century, sumptuary laws became widespread in Italy and elsewhere, the purpose of which was to curb unnecessary spending and lavish displays of clothing and ornamentation, as well as excesses in staging celebrations, banquets, and even funerals. These regulations sought to establish what was defined as a "precise code of appearances."[2] The sumptuary laws logged, with minute fastidiousness, the length of dresses and trains, the colours, number of buttons, and ornaments, etc. to indicate what was allowed and what was not. Where prostitutes were concerned, in some cases, the laws dropped all prohibitions, allowing prostitutes to wear garments forbidden to respectable women, thus perpetuating a division and differentiation that made them stand out and be recognizable. Generally speaking, prostitutes were warned away from living in certain streets next to public buildings or in the vicinity of a place of worship or of a consecrated building, like a monastery. The distance that had to be respected was determined as no less than 200 *braccia* (the length of an arm) and sometimes even 500. Streets that were out of bounds were mostly those of the urban centres but also those that led to the ports or entrance and exit streets because the spectacle of women putting their bodies up for sale would have been inappropriate to those coming into the city from elsewhere, travelling for business, on pilgrimage, or on the way to their country estates. We find the harshest restrictions in the thirteenth century and into the first half of the fourteenth century. Floggings were expected for women found in forbidden locations or in a household brothel. Repeat offenders had their faces marked, on the right cheek, as a sign of additional discrimination and in order to ruin the face, thus devaluing the merchandise.

In Carcassonne and Toulouse, they were exiled to outside the city walls, and not allowed into the city except on a given day of the week. In 1285 in Montpellier it was decided that prostitutes would be assigned to a few streets in Villanova, a suburb of the city. The name of *Carreria calida* was given to the area, but from there, as well, they were soon cast out by the will of the people.[3] In Ferrara, the zones off limits to prostitutes were numerous. The barring of them from within the circle of city walls was practically extended to the entire zone, in an area circumscribed by the four main streets: the via Grande, the via di San Domenico, the via del Terraglio,and the via Nuova. But the prohibitions stretched beyond even the centre, for instance into the northern boroughs of San Leonardo and San Guglielmo, where residential areas had been developed more recently and had already happened around important churches and where there was a convent of Poor Clares and a hospital, thus making the presence of public prostitutes impossible. The prescribed penalties in this case were also very harsh: a flogging for those guilty of an infraction, a fine for the person who had invited them, and the destruction of the house in which they had plied their trade. In Turin, a decree of Duke Amedeus VIII forced all prostitutes within the territory under his dominion to live in an "ignominious and concealed place" far from any possible proximity to decent women. In York in 1301, in a brutally explicit manner, prostitutes were compared to pigs: residence within the city walls was in fact prohibited to the former, and it was here that pigs were also forbidden to move freely.[4]

The constitution of the Municipality of Siena, whose drafting harks back to the first decade of the fourteenth century, established that "no prostitute, madam, or any woman of ill repute, slandered in speech and life" could be or take residence near the Palazzo Pubblico (the public palace), also known as the "house of the governing Council of Nine," or near other municipal buildings except at a distance of no less than two hundred *braccia* (length of an arm). What is more, the women were not authorized to live in any place within the neighbourhood of San Chimenti, from the church of the friars of the Servi di Maria up to the Peruzini Gate and from the said neighbourhood up to the San Maurizio Gate and not even in the so-called *fosso* (trench) or *carbonaia* (charcoal pit), which was situated from the Uvile Plain until the Campansi Gate and where the notary of the *podestà* (chief magistrate) would execute a monthly inspection. The penalty was calculated as a fine of twenty coins or a month in prison. The same body of laws decreed that in the "public avenues and streets" of Siena no one may dare to keep as a tenant or rent a house to thieves, pimps, gambling-house keepers, and prostitutes, equating the latter with felons and criminals.[5] In the 1327 statute of the city of Arezzo, access and residence in the entire city, boroughs, and suburbs were denied to prostitutes, and they were only granted authorization to stay in the building where they usually resided and its vicinity.[6] In the city of

Lucca, the dispositions of the law of 1308, 1331, and 1342 reiterated harsh measures against public prostitutes and pimps, equating them by judgment to "villains" or to blind or physically maimed people, a marginal population not kindly looked upon, in the prohibitions, forcing them to approach the city walls and sacred places at a distance of no less than twice the length of a crossbow shot.[7] Over the course of the fourteenth century in Perugia, regulations gradually became more and more restrictive until the decree, at the close of the century, that every public woman had to "go and stay within the so-called public place of the brothel." Previously, in 1342, prostitutes were forbidden to stay less than the distance of ten houses from the churches of the old city and the boroughs, while in 1359 the space permitted to them earlier had already been reduced to a single area called *Malacucina*.[8]

The spatial distribution of prostitutes in the city was aimed at limiting and distancing displays, judged to be scandalous, from the most sensitive areas of the city with the added intention, not always stated, of also hiding the clients from view, essentially to conceal the commercial transaction, which was judged to be not quite honourable or respectable, for the good name and prestige of the municipalities and governments. Other laws, regarding attire and more, pertained strictly to the persons involved and demonstrated an even more obvious determination to exclude and humiliate. Certain demands on dress and other interdictions weighed heavier than the restriction on residence, which was directed towards avoiding the display of solicitation and the exposure of the vice of lust. They weighed on the person of the public woman and on her activity. Why camouflage, conceal, stigmatize, and label her when her presence was considered useful and necessary as a means to avoid worse evils? Hypocrisy, ambiguity, and the incongruousness of her existence itself can be recognized between the lines of the legal provisions. The prostitute, by nature, is an unnatural contrivance, created for the desires of men, for their pleasure, for the release of their sexual urges. She was considered impure, a sinner, and a corruptor of souls, and yet it was believed that individuals and society could not do without her. She was hidden on the outskirts of the city, outside the circle of the walls that protected the urban community, in the slum neighbourhoods, far from contact with honourable, moral, and virtuous women who represent the other face of womanhood: the wife, mother, sister, and daughter, the woman to be respected and loved. Men – husbands, legislators, clergymen, the powerful, and the humble – see their lust, the weakness of their flesh, the substance itself of their instincts mirrored in the prostitute. They take pleasure in her body when and how they want. They know that she will be amenable to every order and request, docile, and obliging. She has been bought for an hour or a night, purchased as merchandise, an object belonging to the purchaser, provided that it is very evident who she is: a body contaminated by the use of too many men, a body to be identified and pointed out to the attention of all, of those who might wish to avoid such a body, and to those who, on the contrary, might wish to exploit it.

Thus we have a flowering of stripes and fabric, hoods and cloaks, of various sizes and colours: white, yellow, red. In Valencia, it was a short yellow mantilla (scarf), while in Venice, the women wore a handkerchief of the same colour around the neck. In Milan and Pavia, they covered their head, breast, shoulders, and back with a hood and a white cape. In Padua, the hood was red, and in Perugia, the strip of cloth sewn onto the right shoulder was red, three fingers long, and one finger wide. In Marseille, the prescribed cloak was striped, similar to the hood that was worn in London. In Toulouse, on the other hand, the striped hood was white. In Cremona, the short cape was made of white linen, and in Bergamo of yellow fustian.

Some cities added particulars of an insulting nature to these distinguishing signs or clothing items that had become obligatory, such as the extremely high bonnet provided with two horns at least half a foot long, invented by Duke Amadeus VIII of Savoy or the falcon rattle, worn on the shoulder and attached with a band in Siena, or in Florence, the same rattle applied to a hood and made in such a way as to cover the entire head. The rattle was required to sound with scrupulous precision and not remain silent through some clever ploy of the prostitutes. One cannot help but be reminded, in this example of rattles, that lepers, too, were required to make their arrival known by ringing a bell so that the passersby could get out of their way and avoid contact with the disease and the contamination of their flesh. After all, the fact that in Avignon public women could not touch food with their naked hands and that in Florence they were obliged to always wear gloves, had nothing to do with precautions of a hygienic nature (in some cities this obligation was extended to the entire community of customers) but with the conviction or the suspicion or the prejudice or moral stigma that these women were contaminated.[9]

The legislators from Bologna, in relation to the clothes and symbols, punctiliously divided wicked women into two groups: the "indecent ones who are living an evil life, namely the housewives" and the prostitutes "of the public brothel." The former were prohibited from camouflaging themselves and wearing certain types of clothing – above all the wearing of trains – while the shame of wearing a rattle on the shoulder was imposed on the latter, with the usual stipulation that it had to be open and not closed so that it could sound and be clearly visible.[10]

In times of regulation, in which all clothing, masculine and feminine, was subjected to a strict and structured series of prohibitions and restraints, in some municipalities it was precisely the "public prostitutes who surrender their bodies to lust for pecuniary gain" that were exonerated from the most common prohibitions, perhaps in order to allow them to have the trappings of vanity. This type of permissiveness also created a distinction; in any case, they wanted these women to be different from ordinary women and to dress differently. The symbols of inequality remained in force, as well, throughout the fifteenth century, the century in which the desire for normalization and legalization of the phenomenon was strongest.

They persisted unchanged. They surfaced in moments of difficulty. They intensified, subsequent to a movement towards reform, and they closely followed the wave of emotions and reactions triggered by a sermon by some friar, particularly gifted in the art of oratory and the art of crowd persuasion. Nonetheless, during the first decades of the sixteenth century, in conjunction with the partial failure of undertakings to control prostitution and increased pressure from the church and petitions for reform, these symbols came back into effect everywhere. The authorities wished to rein in an unforeseen phenomenon: an increase in clandestine prostitution, which, after a long battle conducted by public authorities to keep it within the reassuring confines of public brothels, had returned to invade the streets.

> It is obvious, most exalted and magnificent Lords … of the city of Florence, how much chaos is created when female prostitutes travel the streets in such a way that they are not distinguishable from the other women and that it would be good to find a remedy for such an inconvenience, for that reason it should be seen to that … they must wear a veil on their head, the size of at least one square *braccia*, and of a red, green, yellow, or pale colour.

The attitude towards the symbol has softened, and even the colour has been left to personal taste and freedom of choice, but the intent remains the same: make sure that the prostitute is recognizable and, above all, distinguishable from God-fearing women of good repute.[11] The royal decrees of Christian Spain, just like municipal ordinances and sumptuary laws, made the goal of such provisions explicitly clear. If public women dress like those who were "honourable and leading a lawful and honest life," by concealing their low status beneath the same cloaks and hoods and clothes, the men seeking them out and following them, uttering indecent and illicit proposals, could make a mistake "from which good women of honour and prominence would take offence and feel outrage, and from which great pain and inconvenience might arise."[12] The adjectives that describe these women are not generically expressive of respectable status but precisely highlight the status of honourable women of good repute and of a high level of social prestige. An insult to them could have engendered a scandal, causing serious problems and substantial consequences.

Inasmuch as legal and clandestine prostitutes were subjected to controls and restrictions on personal freedom, and inasmuch as the population of the brothels consisted of people foreign to the city, they were still a part of the urban microcosm. It was difficult to ignore them, even though one might try to keep one's distance, and enclose them inside separate buildings and locations. It was difficult to manage them without a sense of discomfort, a hint of contradiction, and ambivalence. Jacques Rossiaud indeed maintains, on the basis of particular examples from France and Germany, that some kind of integration of public women was achieved in urban societies, where it was common for them to participate in public festivities and private parties, even of an intimate character like that of a wedding, and where they had occasion to celebrate specific rituals, such as the offering of *focacce* (a type of flatbread) to the municipal authorities and recurring religious observances, such as the glorification of patron saints.[13] In Sicily, prostitutes took part in the 22 July procession in honour of Mary Magdalene, considered to be their patron saint.[14] We have, as well, at least one report of a special festivity within the context of other Italian cities: the *palio* horse race. In the wonderful fresco cycle, unfortunately partially destroyed, on the walls of the hall of honour of the Schifanoia Palace in Ferrara, residence of Sigismondo, the brother of Duke Ercole, there is a representation of the *palio*, an annual race that included, besides horses, also a race between donkeys, one of Jews, and one of prostitutes. Though not represented as strikingly as in the case of the painting, these took place in other cities and on other occasions. In Périgueux and Palermo, in Pavia and in Foligno, a city in which public women, in the middle of the fifteenth century, ran on the occasion of the *palio* of Saint Feliciano from the

Governor's Gate to the Palace of Priors. The fastest woman, she who arrived first, had to grab objects deposited there, a sheaf of hemp, a pound of pepper, and two bundles of leeks, and bring them back.[15] In times of siege the *palio* race included prostitutes running along the ramparts with their skirts raised. Was this intended to show that the inhabitants were not preoccupied in the least, and so treated themselves to amusements, or was it to make fun of the enemy, to laugh at them? It certainly seems difficult to believe that behind this request of the public women to lend themselves, in such a way, to the "game" there could be an intent to involve them in participating in the life of the community. Rather it seems that it was, yet again, a way to humiliate them, out of arrogance, ignorance, and indifference.

7

Public Women and Public Officials

Besides being controlled by the wearing of visible symbols and numerous other prohibitions and regulations, prostitutes, Jews, and lepers were, for a certain amount of time and in certain places, subject to an absurd overturning of roles not unusual in medieval societies: they were ruled by the "king of knaves," also called the "king of charlatans" or "le rey Arlot" in the Kingdom of Valencia. Between the thirteenth and fourteenth centuries in many cities of France and Spain, in Piedmont, Vicenza, and in central Italy, power and control over public prostitutes was entrusted to these figures, recruited by urban governments from among gamblers, dominant in the world of the marginalized, which also included vagrants, pimps, and individuals of the lowest reputation. This "knave" was generally a gambling man, who spent all his time making wagers and did not have regular work, not a respectable or respected person but one who had a certain amount of weight in the criminal world, and in that microcosm of the uprooted and marginalized, a fringe sector of the population, which seemed to live according to different norms and customs than those of the majority. We have here an upside down world upon which an ironic caricature of a sovereign has been imposed, one who is supposed to execute the dispositions of government oriented towards his subjects while functioning as a mediator with civil society. He was called an "inveterate king of charlatans" in Lucca, and this emphatic exaggeration seems to highlight the derision heaped onto the subjects over whom he dominates. In Bologna, this gambling fraudster was known as the *potestas marochorum*, the authority over the *marochi* (the gambling games), a rather ambiguous public responsibility seeing as he was an integrated part of the circle of marginal individuals and yet assigned by the municipality to collect the tariff on the games and to discipline the public behaviour of gamblers as well as that of prostitutes and pimps.

This unusual representative of power – a further sign of scorn towards a hated world – faded out over the course of the fourteenth century in those places in which he had been appointed: in Valencia in 1337, in Lille from around 1334, in Arras much later, after 1441, and in Lucca after 1348. When this special system of control over prostitutes was abandoned, it was necessary to identify which magistracy was the most suitable to replace it, either from the already existing ones or from a newly created one.[1]

Whether they were recent or preexisting, especially in those places where the figure of the "king of knaves" did not prosper or was never adopted, these offices were set up to manage the entity of prostitution in a period of transformation, and they had new tasks and unprecedented difficulties. To begin with, there were relationships with other governing bodies and conflicts around jurisdiction, and then there were the complicated relationships with the prostitutes themselves, with their pimps, and the brothel keepers. It often happened that the officials appointed to a task judged to be ignominious were considered of lesser importance than their more powerful colleagues, almost as if the contempt for the environment under their jurisdiction enveloped them and eventually discredited them as well. This overlapping occurred often for a variety of reasons. The most powerful officials tended to act directly, ignoring related jurisdictions, and availed themselves of the weight and might of their position. Failure to observe jurisdictional autonomies was generated not only by conflicts between the various entities of the state but sometimes by the lack of clarity of the legislative instruments, in which the tasks and areas of intervention, although specified, did not take into account previous duties, or related or even equivalent issues. This depreciation of authority, with the resulting difficulty in imposing obedience, did not only come from above. It was also a significant element within that world that public officials were supposed to monitor, supervise, and manage. Failure to observe rules, announcements, and appeals addressed to superior authorities hindered their work and function, leading to a total lack of respect, insults, even assaults. The predominant interests never seemed to be those for which they had been appointed – the good administration of a complex phenomenon – but rather the particulars of so many others: sometimes it was about privileging influential private citizens, sometimes it was about financial offices, protesting reduced revenues, and sometimes it was about professional corporations in dispute over their own profits. Pressed on one side and the other, at times summoned by the supreme authority, the magistracies were forced to deviate from their proper path and to behave differently from what the laws prescribed. This also affected the results of their management, by interrupting, worsening, and rendering their program of administration disorganized and incoherent. Within this confusion they sometimes lost their way, in terms of personal correctness, arriving perilously close to a conflict of interest, or of accepting complicity and compromises, in disregard of the proper honour of public magistrates.

In France, there were no special officials appointed to deal with the issue of prostitution. In the chain of command, which had the king and his decrees at the top, through to the district judge and his lieutenant, down to the city consuls, the final link was represented by the brothel keeper.

The evolution within the Christian Spanish regime was original, and, as we shall see, some of their solutions were rather unique. In 1337, King Peter IV conferred the power of naming a deputy, to whom was entrusted the entire issue of management and control of prostitutes, upon the magistracy of Criminal Justice. This represented the beginning of a change, first and foremost by marking a shift in jurisdiction from the king to the municipality and second by creating a single key figure for the position. In addition, no distinction was made between men and women: the door to this career was open to women as much as to men. This deputy took the name of *hostaler* (innkeeper) in the Kingdom of Aragon and father or mother of the *mancebías* (brothels) in Castile. He or she was the keeper of the most important brothel and took charge of the entire complex of the houses of prostitution, assuming responsibility for the property and the admission of women into the houses. His or her tasks were many: this person had to collect the taxes owed by the prostitutes, watch over the behaviour of everyone working within the house, impose fines for irregular conduct, maintain the peace within the walls of the brothel, try to contain violence outside its walls, make sure that the women in particular behaved well and did not leave the houses in order to work outside, and that they did not have special friends among the clients. Originally, these deputies may have been the proprietors of illegal private brothels or, among the female deputies, prostitutes themselves, and this constituted the main problem of a system in which the officials assigned to its functioning were themselves individuals of questionable reputation and deeply involved in profitable business dealings. We are not exactly in the sphere of the "king of knaves" and his kingdom, populated with marginal characters and rejects, but almost.

Nevertheless, the originality, and it goes without saying, the unusualness, of the solutions found in Spain is not limited to the function of deputies granted to figures of murky reputation, and above all not possessing the requisites of public officials, and not even to the fact that women were successfully admitted into their ranks. It manifested itself in subsequent years in some of the provisions of Isabella and Ferdinand. With the *Reconquista* virtually at an end – only

Granada still endured – the very Catholic sovereigns no longer knew how to reward the vassals who had fought so long and valiantly by their side. It seems that there were no more free tracts of land available to hand over as fiefdoms, and so in 1486 the Catholic regents gave to Alonso Yáñez Fajardo, in exchange for services rendered, the right of exploitation of all brothels, including those of the not yet conquered kingdom of Granada. Alonso thus became *el señor de las mancebías* (the lord of the brothels) from 1486 to 1496, and his descendants, down to the last one in 1539, inherited the title. This seems to be a truly strange sovereignty and a bizarre recognition – a sort of overturning of the noble values of chivalry and loyalty to the king. Honoured with these outlandish titles, the new deputies did not show repugnance towards benefitting financially from a business based on the commercialization of women's bodies. The elevated world of the aristocracy and the bourgeoisie were in absolute harmony with the lowly world of the marginalized.

García de Abarrastigui, crossbowman to the king, received the concession of the bordello of Salamanca, while Pedro Madrazo, a member of the royal horse guards to whom the *mancebías* of Cuenca were given as reward, found himself deprived of his rights by the municipality, which, in 1494, chose Bernaldina Rodriguez over him. She was already the keeper of a city brothel, where she employed women "que ganaban dineros con su cuerpo" (who earned their living with their bodies). Seeing himself divested of a rich source of income, Pedro sought help from sovereign authority and won his argument after quite a few years. In 1512, by order of Queen Joanna, the municipality had to pay him the sum of 25,000 *maravedís*, the ancient Spanish coins in use between the twelfth and nineteenth centuries. In the meantime, Bernaldina had defended her own monopoly, presenting her argument not only to the military favoured by the royals but also to the Hospital of San Jorge, an institution of significant weight in the life of the citizens, where she declared to have inherited rights to the brothels from a certain Tereçia la Cucharera, having helped her during a period of contagion. Bernaldina Rodriguez continued to ensure her dominion over the brothels to her own family and descendants.[2] Furthermore, even where this unusual way of rewarding loyalty on the part of the sovereigns did not exist, wealthy and self-righteous citizens did not refrain from renting out their own houses to brothelkeepers, regretting the decision only due to missed payments, the desertion of the buildings on the part of the renters without having settled their debts, and the almost impossible likelihood of rerenting those buildings considering the state of ruin in which they were left.

During the fourteenth and fifteenth centuries, in the majority of cases and cities, especially Italian ones, the control of prostitution was assigned to an already existing magistracy, one with duties that seemed the closest match. It was entrusted less frequently to a new institution, created on purpose, mostly to coincide with innovative projects of tolerance and institutionalization. In Siena, the delegation of the control and application of the laws to a specific official was motivated by the fact that the mechanisms against "pimps, prostitutes, and women of ill repute and low status" were not being executed. To this end a "superior examining Judge" of the city, who would have by his side a notary and the relevant *berrivieri* (mercenary policemen, usually foreign), was appointed. The reason identified for the nonapplication of regulations was the fact that a multitude of trials had overburdened the courts of the *Podestà* (the highest magistrate), making it unable to adequately solve the matter.[3]

In Bologna, between the end of the thirteenth century and the beginning of the fourteenth, the *Ufficio corone e armi*, the entity responsible for the supervision of gambling along with other tasks, was also entrusted, because of certain similarities, with monitoring prostitution. The office, an organism of the justice court, was presided over by a notary of the *podestà* and had jurisdiction over sumptuary issues. Furthermore, his duties also included those involved with the maintenance of public order, with the added task of checking for the presence of women of ill repute within urban parishes where they were banned. By the end of the fourteenth century, the officials of the treasury (*delle Bollette*), who were delegated to police foreigners and collect taxes on immigrants, came under the magistracy of the *Corone e armi*. In the 1442 statutes of Bologna, we find the addition of another section to their list of duties, "De lupanarii meretricibus et lenonibus" (that of the brothels, prostitutes, and pimps). Thus the scope of their intervention was extended.[4] The addition of the issue of prostitution to this particular judicial branch was not unusual or odd. In some Italian cities it seemed to be the most suitable set up, since their sphere of interest already focussed on an "alien" population, sometimes even undesirable, towards whom it was necessary to adopt cautionary measures and provide methods of assessing their origins, objectives, lengths of stay, and grant a safe-conduct pass for their stay within the city walls, once the admissibility conditions had been certified. The intention was to check, and possibly avoid, the access of criminals, vagrants, the marginalized without employment, and without sources of income to the city. The prostitutes and pimps were mostly foreigners and strangers to the communities in which they worked and therefore could be assimilated into the itinerant population, and signify a similarity of context in terms of the monitoring of their activities by the appropriate officials.

In Ferrara, the capital of the d'Este state, this assignment was given to the office of the treasury (*delle Bollette*) as well, with an actual transfer of powers taking place on 24 July 1438. Previously, from 1371 and by means of an agreement between Nicholas II and the magistracy of the XII Sages (the entity governing the municipality) this task was administered by the officials of the *Gabella grande* or *di Piazza* (the tax officials), namely those who took care of all merchandise manufactured or sold in the city. Prostitutes, according to the logic of assigning duties to comparable areas of operation, were thus considered consumer goods. With the entrusting of the issue of prostitution to new officials through a letter from the marquis, an amended compilation of laws was drawn up. To the multiple tasks that they previously undertook, such as the monitoring of strangers and foreigners in the city, the granting of transit and residence permits, the granting of licences to innkeepers, tavern keepers, and hoteliers, and the suppression of gambling, was added that of overseeing, judging, and punishing prostitutes and pimps. The office was led by two superiors, guarantors of civil and penal justice administration, some notaries responsible for the keeping of records and the granting of "passes" to travellers from outside the city, and one or more members tasked with "policing" and inspecting. These latter were tasked with patrolling streets, taverns, and inns while checking for possible infractions of the laws. The officials had the right to bear arms, day and night, to capture and imprison prostitutes, and to punish them if they refused to reside in the dwelling assigned to them. They were allowed to knock at any time on the door of the residences of prostitutes, who were obliged to answer immediately, and to open chests and coffers within the establishment, and withdraw the money perhaps owed for taxes or fines.

Nevertheless, already from the beginning, these prerogatives seemed open to extensive overlapping in terms of jurisdiction and caused friction and disputes as well as acts of intrusiveness on the part of different officials. In the meantime, the control, for instance, of women's scandalous behaviour, aimed at restraining the behaviour of prostitutes, had come under the purview of another civic functionary: the bailiff of the neighbourhoods. Moreover, due to their very nature, crimes against morality, and all crimes within this context, lay within the authority of the judge of malevolent conduct, who intervened in cases of incest, rape, abduction, corruption of women, adultery, bigamy, sodomy, and, before the fifteenth century, interdictions on the residency of prostitutes in certain districts of the city. The statutes themselves fostered confusion instead of ending the tangle of contradictory regulations, making it necessary in quite a few cases to resort to the supreme authority of the Lord of the House of Este. A few years after the 1438 decree of Nicholas III, it had already become evident that in some cases the powers conferred upon this magistracy were uncertain because of the fact that prostitutes and pimps were being accused and brought to justice before tribunals, different from the one in which they were supposed to be judged, according to the statutes in effect. This was not about a protest based on pure motives of jurisdiction. Underlying the situation were very specific interests. One episode, which took place in 1447, sheds a very realistic light on the whole scene. There occurred within the city an en masse exodus of pimps, and the fifteen who had remained felt it necessary to present a detailed complaint outlining the reasons for the distress. On 25 June they turned to the marquis informing him of having been subjected to judges and tribunals other than the established ones and to have been burdened with excessive fines, "nimias extorsiones" (exorbitant exactions), and harsh convictions, whereas the punishments dispensed by the magistracy of the *Bollette* (the treasury) were considered extremely light. To what can we impute this difference and relative indulgence on the part of the officials of the *Bollette*? Was it a conspiracy? Was it tolerance? Was it due to better knowledge of that world and of the reduced economic capacity of those operating within it? In any case, one fact is certain: With this complaint, as with others, nothing was done except to reiterate the weakness of the judiciary, bringing to light its impotence, in relation to colleagues with greater power.

In the summer of 1469 there was another event with subsequent conflicts of interest and magistracies involving many state organisms, and at the forefront Duke Borso. On 11 July, the officials of the Bollette convicted a prostitute who "et facevasi tochare in una hostaria da le volte. Similiter uno hosto che sta in dicto (et era rufiano) et dava recepto a tale meretrice" ("sometimes allowed herself to be touched in a tavern. Similarly, a tavern keeper, as it has been asserted (and he was a pimp), gave admission to this prostitute"). The magistrate had the right and reason to impose the monetary penalty, since, according to the statutes, public women could not spend time in a tavern, not even to eat. Therefore, he registered the sentence at the office of the Ducal Chamber. However, the general administrators (those defending economic interests, "li generali factori") upon whom the Chamber depended prohibited the collection of the amounts, at the request of the wine tax officials and, perhaps, of others not clearly specified. They feared, in fact, that by prohibiting the presence of prostitutes in those places where one ate and most especially drank, there would be a reduction in consumption and consequently in revenues flowing into the coffers of the state. The authorities responsible for the control of prostitution became irritated and wrote a letter of remonstrance to the duke. In the letter they asked how they were supposed to understand their function: "If you would please advise us, if it is of your mind that the statutes and orders of our office serve perfectly or that we agree to the will of the general administrators, setting aside the statutes and our orders, so that we know how to govern ourselves in the future."

In short, and perhaps with a hint of impatience while proudly defending their authority, the officials wished to know from the lord what his actual intentions were and how they should behave in future: obey the law or allow the economic interests of others to prevail. Duke Borso hastily responded, calling them "dilectissimi nostri" (our cherished ones), praising their work, and inviting them to always observe the statutes.[5] But the annoyance manifested by these officials, and the undue interference on the part of their colleagues, most probably expressing, at least in part, the requests of the tavern and inn keepers, represented divergent interests in the social fabric of the city and even in the apparatus of the state. On the one hand, we have the will to control and respect for law codified in the statutes, and on the other, there were the economic interests, to the benefit of those involved in the selling and consuming of wine, of those in the sex market and those pressing for an unequivocal indulgence towards financial organisms always engaged in filling the ducal coffers.

Discontent over conflicts in responsibilities did not only concern the more noble aspects, namely the dignity of the office and respect for the authority of the appointees. Perhaps it concealed a less noble side. In fact, for every case judges collected a sum of money, and their salary was also established upon the number of cases debated. Thus, judiciaries competed, to a certain extent, with each other, a consideration made more significant considering that payment occurred subject to a system of *sportule* (gifts): contributions proportionate to the contested sum of money, the duration of the case, and the social status of the accused person. The calling into question of authority, in particular that of the officials of the *Bollette*, whose decisions were contested and often annulled without reason, undermined the prestige of this office and ended up causing reverberations throughout the microcosm of prostitution. Those who inhabited it were prompted to believe that it was not absolutely necessary to obey, and that this magistracy, deprived of any real power, did not deserve respect. Pimps, keepers, and prostitutes adopted an attitude of challenge, without fear or regard for this authority. They had no consideration nor did they fear the consequences of their insolent behaviour.

On 27 July 1491, we have a random example of this. The associated sitting judiciary had to examine a dispute between a prostitute and a certain Nardo, at one time her protector, who had illegally taken possession of some of her articles and had no intention of returning them. When he was officially summoned, the man in question behaved so irreverently, using such indecent language, "acti bestiali" (beastly deeds), and with an attitude so antagonistic and "fulminoso" (fierce) as to cause the officials to pray to God to give them "bona bona patientia" (good good patience) towards him.[6] Nardo's insolence and his lack of respect and deference towards the state's representatives may have come from the fact that he belonged to the entourage that had arrived in the city, a while before, accompanying Eleanor of Aragon on the occasion of the wedding of Ercole d'Este. Even if this man had been transformed into the exploiter and protector of women that he had become, he obviously still presumed to have some protection at court. However, others as well, pimps and prostitutes, often behaved towards officials with unrestrained arrogance. One of the numerous privileges, at the disposal of these officials, was that they could inspect, at any hour of the day or night, the residences of prostitutes, who were required to allow them immediate entry, and if they did not comply, could be fined. But often they refused to comply, or, once they obeyed, insulted and blasphemed the inspectors. The magistracies in charge of prostitution had to deal from all sides with an undisciplined world, whose inhabitants were little inclined to follow the norms, used direct and coarse language, and unabashedly disregarded the consequences of their behaviour.

In Florence, a new entity was created with great ceremony and explicit declarations of intent. It was in April 1403 that the priors took decisive measures to bring under control the phenomenon of prostitution, with a conviction to combat the "heinous crime of sodomy," and the "depravity of the abominable vice" contrary to nature. The goal was therefore to combat male homosexuality through the supervision and institutionalization of prostitution. The actual birth of the office had to wait about decade. It was only in 1415 that it became operational, with a specific statute that regulated its composition, function, and duties. Appointed biannually, eight popular Guelph citizens (supporters of the pope), two per neighbourhood, and a notary were supposed to take on this task. Their chosen name was that of "ufficiali dell'Onestà" (officers of Decency), motivated not so much out of irony, of which Florentine governors were masters, but rather out of a basic aspiration towards honest and fair management, even of something disreputable – a cornerstone of the moralizing politics of the fifteenth century. Within the first thirty years of the fifteenth century, the Florentine republic had in fact instituted some new magistracies, with the common characteristic of having specific jurisdiction over crimes against morality. Initially, the responsibility of choosing a suitable location for the building of a brothel was entrusted to the Office of Decency. Later it was tasked with authorizing the presence of public prostitutes and their pimps, with deciding on the symbols to enforce, and the tariffs to exact for the service, with granting licences and safe-conduct passes, with receiving oaths of allegiance and exchanges of promises, with preparing cases for trial, and with inflicting penalties, whether of a financial or punitive character. In other words, the Office of Decency was to become the filter between the microcosm of the marginalized and the city, the instrument of good government within the lowly world of deviant individuals, foreigners, and strangers, people without respectable work. Their goal towards the prostitutes, in particular, was to provide justice, equably distributing punishment and protection. Once subjected to the jurisdiction of the Onestà, the latter were exempt from that of any other deputy or official. The only crime excluded from all possible forms of immunity was that of rebellion against the Florentine state.[7]

During their term of action, the officials of the Onestà were, however, hindered by other magistrates, who in part overlapped with them in terms of duties, as did the *podestà* (the highest authority), or who were simply more powerful and with such a wide field of jurisdiction that they acted brazenly and without respecting the boundaries of their colleagues' jurisdiction. Furthermore, since the people referred to the Office of Decency were of low status, special care was not used when apprehending them, even when the behaviour of the officials was contrary to the form of the law, unless an actual crime was committed during the intervention. This is what happened in the case of the Hungarian John of Pest, an attendant to the *podestà*, who, after apprehending a German prostitute named Margaret threatened her by drawing his sword, thus violating the bounds of his authority.[8] Conflicts with the office of the *podestà* were commonplace, and during the decades that the Office of Decency existed it was difficult to compete for space with the magistracy of the Eight, who were in charge of public order. As was customary, the officials had to make efforts to protect the good name of the office by suppressing challenging attitudes and disobedience on the part of public prostitutes, as well as insolence, abuse, and insults from the pimps, who heaped discredit on their office.

PART THREE

The Places and the Rules

8

Loca inhonesta (The House of Ill Repute)

Once European cities decided to establish public brothels to accommodate prostitutes, exhorting them not to practice their "art" elsewhere, local governments took a series of initiatives in order to regulate and control the procedures. Timetables and methods were not harmonized or uniform. From the end of the thirteenth century, throughout all of the fourteenth, and up to the first decades of the fifteenth, documentary evidence yields an image of a sequence of initiatives. In France, Christian Spain, Italy, and Germany brothels were built, houses of ill-repute were refurbished, run-down houses were renovated, others not considered of sufficient size were extended, and neighbourhoods and streets where sexual commerce was to be segregated were identified.

The Montpelier project in France was among the earliest to create a neighbourhood destined exclusively for prostitution. It was 1285 and all the prostitutes of the city were forced to move into that district and settle there permanently. They did not have permission to leave it. In Burgundian Dijon, the space reserved for prostitution was instead organized into a brothel, which opened in 1385, and early on was revealed to be inadequate, forcing the authorities to set up another house beside it, at the beginning of the next century. Whether in one form or the other, their example was followed by numerous other urban centres in the kingdom.[1]

In Christian Spain, the process seemed to lag in comparison with the French development. Even though it was legislated from the thirteenth century in the regions of Léon and Castile, the institution of the municipal bordello in the cities was delayed for a few decades. In Valencia, it was present by the middle of the fourteenth century. Elsewhere, as in Segovia, documentation attests to its appearance only from 1478.[2]

Italy, within the various states that composed it, was provided early on with specific legislation and furnished spaces. Turin, Milan, Venice, Ferrara, Florence, Pisa, Lucca, Pistoia, Siena, Perugia and a few cities in the peninsular south, and in the insular south, as in Palermo, built public brothels, often segregated by a walled-in boundary or set up well-identified zones into which prostitutes were channelled and forbidden to leave. Gian Galeazzo Visconti, Lord of Milan, invited the municipality in December 1390 to transform the place in which lewd women habitually resided into a "separate place, enclosed by a wall, entrusted to the custody of a keeper, provided with a set of keys to close the gate in the evening, and reopen it in the morning."[3]This invitation was readily accepted, and the following January the municipality began the construction of a walled-in enclosure in the neighbourhood of San Giacomo de Raude. Seven years later the wall, which had fallen, was rebuilt. By the decree of Amedeus VIII, Duke of Savoy, enacted on 17 June 1430, the prostitutes of Turin were forced to live in a remote and poor area, of little value and hidden from the sight of decent women; the following year the municipality purchased a house in the same area and fitted it out as a brothel. A few years later, however, the building was on the verge of collapse, and it was necessary to make urgent repairs.[4]

The Venetian Grand Council, when it met in 1358, initiated the process of reorganizing prostitution. St Augustine was the source of inspiration for the legislation: "Female sinners are absolutely indispensable to the Earth," stated the politicians of Venice, in total harmony with the opinion expressed by the religious thinker. Proceeding, although slowly, with the plan, two years later they first selected an area in the Rialto district, and later, after more than ten years, on 15 December 1369, some houses near San Matteo, on the island of Rialto, were designated the location of the sex trade. It was given the name *castelletto* (small castle), which allows us to surmise the existence of a walled-in enclosure, entrusted in an innovative way to the management of female madams under the supervision of district administrators.[5]

By the first half of the fourteenth century, the municipal government of Siena was paying the rent on houses, positioned in three points of the city, to accommodate prostitutes, and in 1415, they moved the Val di Montone brothel, one of the three, because "the place, which is presently behind the palace is an embarrassment to the palace, and the youth do not go there out of the shame of being seen." Moreover, via a decision taken by the general council, the election of six citizens was ordered. They were to "have full authority and care in providing for a place or places where they would believe it to be more useful for pimps and prostitutes to be … where the youth could more honourably go."[6]

In the south of Italy, in the first three decades of the fifteenth century, the inspiration and models followed, on the legislative level as well, came from the Spanish crown of Aragon. Through the will of Alfonso, sovereign of the Kingdom of Naples, Palermo entrusted its faithful subject Puccio di Simone of Messina to construct a *lupanare* (brothel), beginning in October 1432, in accordance with regulations issued the previous year in Barcelona.[7] In Germany's urban centres, the movement toward brothels proceeded early on, and they opened in the middle of the thirteenth century.

These programs, even if not simultaneous, reveal a commonality of intention tackling the phenomenon of prostitution in countries that were very different from each other in terms of political and economic structure. Is it possible that reports from professional travellers, merchants, coachmen, sailors, and news contained in the missives of ambassadors had transmitted information regarding this embarrassing subject?

Was there an exchange of knowledge that influenced political plans and decisions? Without doubt, governments did not ignore what was happening around them, in the states along their borders, and in more distant lands. Even without discussing these issues, they were informed of the laws, customs, and aspects of administrative life outside their own borders, and it is not inconceivable to think that a wave of intercommunication, in terms of experiments and experiences, cascaded over the Europe of old.

Whatever the date when states instituted residences dedicated to prostitution, there were two types of architectural and spatial models, with a few variants in the interior, commonly used. The most common was probably that of a facility, built or remodelled, in an isolated location, surrounded by a perimeter fence that encircled an open space, a courtyard, and sometimes a garden. The boundary was outwardly marked and the separation symbolically and concretely well defined. These confines were often delineated in a more rigid way by a wall that made the enclosure similar to a fortress, underscoring the element of segregation and otherness: a centre equipped and defended within the city walls, which in turn defended the city from external attacks. The second model did not envisage a single building devoted to the activity nor did it include a surrounding physical barrier that highlighted its purpose and separateness. This model was spread over streets and crossroads, in rooms, studios, and scattered dwellings chosen to house prostitutes. So it was, for instance, in Avignon where a long street ran through the Bourg Neuf, intersected by some side streets, and along which, in buildings both large and small, the prostitutes lived, and baths and taverns were opened.[8] The presence of taverns was not forbidden, and the authorities could not prevent the proximity of family dwellings or artisan workshops, which had nothing to do with prostitution, thus once again mixing the life of common people with a business destined to generate dissatisfaction and discontent. It often happened, however, that little by little ordinary folk departed these areas, leaving some buildings empty, with the result that eventually entire neighbourhoods became reconfigured as zones reserved for the sex trade.

Medieval German bordellos were modelled, structurally and architecturally, according to the example of Roman houses of prostitution containing a large central room and many small single rooms. In the first phase, moreover, they were found in the heart of the city, near the most vital centres of the community – the market, church, well, and central fountain. Only in the second phase, almost diametrically opposed to what other European nations were doing, were the buildings moved outside of city centres, actually outside the walls.[9]

The Valencia model represented a sort of fortified citadel, built in an isolated corner of the city and crossed by four streets. Within it, 150 little houses, painted white and illuminated at night by torches at every doorway, were inhabited by the prostitutes. The only way into the area was through the outer walls, guarded day and night, where the gallows were erected like a warning for both patrons and residents.[10] In the Kingdoms of Aragon and Castile, high, thick masonry walls were built around other bordellos. In the middle of the sixteenth century, organized prostitution in Barcelona was accommodated in a long narrow street, closed off at the end by a large gate that was locked at night, reminding one of the enclosed ghettos created in some cities at the end of the same century to isolate Jews. On the sides of the alleyway, the ground floor rooms of the buildings were lined up like the cells of a monastery or convent. That was where the prostitutes lived and worked. They were similar to the workshops of fifteenth-century Florence. Previously in Barcelona, however, there had been two brothels similar to hotels and with distinguishing features.

Conversely, in France the fenced off public bordellos did not have the threatening and fortified aspect of those in the Spanish city. In Perpignan, the enclosure contained gardens, groves, houses with rooms, reception areas, and even separate bedrooms, all built in the shape of small pavilions: in descriptions, a sort of pleasant place for which it is difficult to attach words and concepts like violence, exploitation, and commodification. The fenced in area of Lyon accommodated houses, gardens, granaries, and was equal to a productive factory, while Toulouse built various buildings, houses, and isolated rooms in its spacious but enclosed Château Vert, which the bordello was called. And Dijon, from 1446, offered a beautiful building with courtyard, portico, and garden to its citizens and passing travellers. Constructed on two floors, linked by a staircase with a balustrade, it included ten rooms and two arcades per floor, a reception room, and a rear hall.[11]

Italian cities, generally speaking, adopted both models. If Milan chose to enclose the brothel with a surrounding wall, Venice and Pisa, by calling the area a "small castle," seem likewise to hint at a fenced-in place, even though the former city offered a group of houses on the island of Rialto and the latter many buildings, with annexes, courts, and orchards.[12] Florence dedicated an extremely central location to prostitution, between two buildings, one a symbol of religious power and the other of civic – the Duomo (the cathedral) and the Palazzo della Signoria (the town hall) – without any kind of boundary wall. The spatial boundary was, if anything, figuratively furnished by a narrow circle of bell towers belonging to the Churches of San Cristofano (or Cristoforo), San Tommaso, Sant'Andrea, Santa Maria Maggiore, San Leo, San Ruffillo, and San Salvatore, which enclosed two nuclei reserved for prostitution. Organized between the streets of chiasso di Malacucina, chiasso Grande, via della Macciana, and chiasso dei Buoi, they consisted of an assemblage of buildings united under the common name of Macciana, a brothel-hotel, and two other hotels called the Frascato, linked to each other by a network of some streets on which there was an array of workshops "suitable for the business of public women." Around the Church of Santa Maria Maggiore, and a short distance away, the street of chiasso dei Buoi contained humble homes and shops inhabited by prostitutes.[13] Inside this area, there were houses belonging to eminent Florentine families, the Medici family, the Pecori family, the della Tosa family, and the Brunelleschi family, and they were modified to become houses of prostitution.

In Venice, the small castle built as a brothel, in the parish of San Matteo di Rialto, had its origins in a group of houses owned by two patrician families, the Venier and the Morosini families, and when, a century later, these houses were in a state of ruin, it was necessary to find another solution. Again the houses of an aristocrat, Priamo Malipiero, were chosen to be used for this purpose.[14] Towards the end of the fifteenth century in Ferrara, where the brothels of Gambero and Santa Croce had already been working for a while, Giacomo Prisciani, a general administrator of Duke Ercole d'Este, also of a higher status than the Office of the Gabelle (the Office of taxes on foodstuffs), wrote to Duchess Eleonora, recounting to her the seriousness of the phenomenon of prostitution, which had become by then uncontrollable. He described Ferrara as "the most plentiful and well-provided in public prostitutes who live an immoral life, causing displeasure and discomfort to those who deplore the life of ill-repute." In order to mitigate the discomfort of respectable people he suggested the construction of a "public place" in addition to the existing buildings. The letter was dated 27 February 1491, but it must not have had the desired effect because Prisciani wrote again the following May, and this time directly to the duke. He referred to "grievances and complaints" because the prostitutes "were scattered all over" in Ferrara in such a disorderly way that it was a great cause of chagrin to the city itself. It was necessary, in his opinion, to compel prostitutes – those women who wished to live "immorally off of their own bodies," as he specified – to live only in the public bordello. He proposed a building with at least twenty-five rooms, "comfortable for such a profession," and hypothesized a cost of 30,000 lire. According to his calculations, however, that sum would be easily repaid by the resulting money that would flow into the ducal coffers. In fact, he predicted an income of at least 50 lire per year for the rental of each room, hinting at a plan that would entail advance payment from interested parties and which would cover a significant portion of the expenses.[15]

The circumstances controlling the life and work of public women were not only dependant on the established regulations of each bordello and on their relationships with keepers, clients, and prospective pimps but also on the actual complexes, on the relative comfortableness of the places, on the state of the dwellings destined for them, and on the furnishings available to them, on their diet, and on the clothes often directly provided by the their overseers. In this regard, the differences seem pronounced, and the evidence at times describes quite decent, even pleasant and attractive situations. Other times, they offer instead, in our view, perspectives of desolation and squalor. Probably the sources, in each of these cases, should be interpreted in a measured way and perhaps trimmed of some exaggerations. The brothel of Valencia, for instance, with its look of a walled fortification, its well-fortified front door, and the gallows visible on the outside, would inspire one to imagine a certain gloom and foreboding, but stories about it describe it as lit up with colours, congeniality, and warmth. The little white well-kept houses, with patios in front, decorated with flowers and aromatic shrubs, and at night illuminated by the flame of torches, evoke a pleasing place of pleasure. They were decorated with taste, like the rooms in the central building, and furnishings, bed linens, pillows, and blankets appeared to be in good condition and possessed some elegance.[16]

The front door of the "great house" of Strasbourg bore a suggestive inscription: "This house is in the hands of God; this is a saying of happy young men." And in Pamiers, the bordello was called Chastel-Joyeux (Happy Castle). Happiness, joy, and lightheartedness are evoked. The names, at least in some European locations, hint at these positive impressions. They inspire us to believe in the existence of places that were well governed and presentable, dedicated to a varied public made up not only of workers, soldiers, and people belonging to the middle to lower classes. Jacques Rossiaud is convinced of this, particularly given that these structures and areas were under the protection of the prince or the lord of the municipality and managed by careful overseers whose main interest was to make the business profitable, increase the earnings, and, therefore, present a tempting, attractive, and highly seductive offering of women and objects: a veritable abode of pleasure, inside of which all the senses were stimulated – sight, smell, and touch. There, clients ate well, drank well, requested a woman for minutes, an hour, or for an entire night to be at their service, a slave to satisfy every desire.[17] According to the French scholar, the brothels were provided with plenty of equipment in the kitchen. The largest structures had a cook, and the women who worked there were generously fed. In Überlingen, as in Ulm, Granada, or Toulouse, twice a day they ate meals that included meat along with a cabbage or turnip soup, and fish and eggs with side dishes on days of abstinence. Moreover, they consumed wheat bread, cheese, and fruit. In 1462, in Toulouse, their diet was established by an ordinance. "Each day, the keeper provides four meals, in other words, in the morning at breakfast, various fried foods or pies; at lunch, boiled or roasted meat, and for snack, something tasty; at dinner, other good foods, and always good wines, reds, whites, and clarets."[18]

Not everywhere, however, was the brothel such a pleasant, orderly, clean, and well kept place. For almost the whole of the fifteenth century, members of the Medici family in Florence passed on, from father to son, the ownership of a hotel and three *botteguzze ne' lluogho chomune* (three small workshop-studios in the common area), meaning the brothel, and the income acquired from the rental of this real estate. Bernardo di Alamanno di messer Salvestro de' Medici, in 1427 and again in 1451, reported in his tax declaration about the constant difficulties in drawing a steady income, as he wrote, "you are renting to Germans, people who are flawed and who provide no security," since, in truth, he suffered many misfortunes with them. One of them departed, stealing the furnishings, resulting, what with the robbery and unpaid rent, in a loss of one hundred florins, a very sizeable sum. Moreover, the houses had been rented for an entire year, during which time it had not been possible to collect any revenue from them.[19] For his son, Iacopo, heir to his assets, it did not go any better. In two successive reports, from 1480 and 1498, he complained that these properties had been the ruin of their house: "for the reason that the innkeepers, who stay there, are foreigners who have nothing. And when one and the other flee, and they take with them the rent money, and sell the furnishings, in such a way, that I can truthfully swear that the said hotel gives me nothing, but rather takes from my own house," and that, furthermore, "they are nothing if not thieves and scoundrels those who want to lease the house."[20]

Another noteworthy family of the city, the della Tosa family, had real estate assets let out for the exploitation of prostitution: a house, "namely a tower," two other houses, with several small houses "attached at the back," from which they reported that they had earned practically nothing. Indeed it cost them to set things right, due to the bad debts, and the ruined condition of the buildings, just about ready to collapse. For these reasons, the della Tosa brothers begged the officials of the Florentine real estate registry to consider the kind of people, with whom they had to deal: "pimps, Germans, Spaniards, the newest kind of sleazy person that you have ever seen" and to be lenient with them when applying taxes.[21] And again in 1480, the heirs of Guidaccio Pecori wrote in their declaration about the revenues from their two "little studios and a half located in the neighbourhood of San Salvatore in Florence, a place called Malachucina … rented for three years…and when they were rented, they were rented month by month … to the pimps who take off with the rent money, and then you end up with nothing."[22] The purpose of the complaints and the descriptions, revealing the devaluation of the assets and income, was without doubt to gain leniency and understanding from the treasury officials in order to obtain a significant reduction in taxes. The descriptions, however, were dramatically realistic. The city's aristocracy did not feel any restraint in conducting business with people belonging to the world of prostitution, except to then complain about lost revenues and to declare that these were due to wicked, dishonest, and foreign individuals devoid of all scruples. Actually, once it was established where the public bordello was to be built or identified, and which shops and houses were to be granted to the prostitutes, all the houses in the vicinity incurred a devaluation. It was inevitable that the only persons willing to take them would be members of that particular microcosm. It would have been otherwise, had influential Florentines, although eventually disillusioned, not pursued a plan to enrich themselves via the disreputable business of prostitution.

The complaints about the state of ruinous squalor into which their properties had descended by the Florentine owners of houses, shops, and hotels "for the use of prostitutes" would demonstrate the contrary of what was happening in other places. It does not appear that those brothel keepers in Florence, mostly insolvent foreigners who disappeared before the end of their contracts without honouring the terms of payment, while actually stripping the places of all furnishings, and reducing them to a pitiable state, by stealing sheets and furniture, actually resembled their Spanish, French, and German colleagues. Given that in the medieval period we do not find a hierarchy of brothels, as we do in contemporary society, we can infer that the association with and use of prostitutes was undifferentiated and not subject to divisions of class, whether we are dealing with comfortable and attractive or much less comfortable quarters. Even though, for example, in Pistoia (also in Tuscany) the appointees of the municipality, the respectable Opera of San Jacopo (Saint James), specifically recommended to the winner of the brothel contract, located next to the market square called la Sala, to provide for the maintenance of the roof of the house "and make sure it did not rain inside," they would not argue in favour of a building in excellent condition. The Opera itself, moreover, had taken on the task of acquiring and constructing within the brothel five or six small rooms that, at the moment of the drafting of the contract, were not yet present.[23] Small workshops, little rooms, *fondachetti* (small storehouses): the terms that in Tuscany allude to the permanent dwellings of the prostitutes make one think more of the humbleness of certain premises rather than the comfort of the amenities and the pleasantness of the places.

In terms of the documented furnishings for some of these settings, they almost never constituted a complete ensemble of accoutrements: a "bedstead" with a "sorry mattress," a "dismal looking blanket and two feather pillows" for sleeping and "working"; a small chest with only one lock, in which to put personal clothing and other little things; a small bench set up next to a table supported on three legs, as well as a trivet, a skillet, and a cauldron represent an assemblage of furnishings, which, if not rich, is at least sufficient. For that matter, as we well know, the quantity of consumer goods was limited compared to current societies, and even homes of well-to-do individuals were equipped with few indispensible objects and furniture. In the shop-style brothel, bedsteads, benches, tables, and chests, in good or not that good condition, furnished a room, with the addition of disparate objects, at times a hutch for storing grain or meal, a jar, two small bottles of vinegar, "a hutch for cheese," "two cages for chickens," a bucket, and two benches for sitting. Sometimes there was only a cane frame with a straw mattress on top or a pallet with a small mattress. The luxury of a curtain above the bed and a bedspread would make one think of objects of a personal character, perhaps accumulated over the course of a few years, rather than of what was allotted and included within the rental of the premises. We would also be prompted to think in this way about the small painted panel of the image of the Virgin Mary, listed among inventoried objects, an unusual presence in a chamber of sin, where lust dominated. It represented perhaps the product of a special devotion and personal feelings, on the part of someone, who still hoped and believed in the benevolence of the Mother, in spite of a life that led her elsewhere.[24]

It is possible that the differences between the structures that we have so far looked into may be a result of diverse types of testimonies. In some cases they are narrative sources, literature, and accounts of trips that offer us attractive descriptions, so evocative as to seem visibly alive but perhaps, in part, deceptive because of the emphasis on the story or the subjectivity in the telling. In others, instead, the nature of the act of documenting confers on the source a dryer, more meagre character and, one could say, objectively more probative. And yet, in the case of the Florentine documents, which show the other side of things, that of the more desolate and degrading of the public spaces, the fact that they are fiscal declarations would lead one to surmise, with some prudence, their complete veracity.

The structures in which public women were confined – to keep them at the disposal of male desire and to avoid their scattering elsewhere in cities inhabited by respectable people – besides having a different look, depending on where they were in Europe, also had managerial styles that were somewhat distinctive. A first discriminating feature was represented by the direct or indirect style of management. In some cases, municipalities ceded rights to the brothel to the highest bidder, for a rather short period of time, receiving, in exchange, an annual rental fee, which had to be paid in advance in one instalment or over several instalments. The winner of the contract would in turn charge the prostitutes rent on the rooms and what was spent on food, sometimes the house linens, and their clothes. The details of these agreements also showed divergences, as we shall see. The winner of the contract would also gain revenue from any taverns within the structure and from the sale of wine and food.

The Venetian government maintained direct management over the public bordello, entrusting its direction to madams (women brothel keepers) recognized to carry out the mandate and who were regularly registered at the office of district chiefs. Financial issues were resolved through the institution of a joint cash pool into which each madam deposited payments turned over by the prostitutes and which was managed by the staff of the municipality, drawing rent from it as well as the salaries of staff, and taking care of the distribution of what was left among the prostitutes.[25] In Pistoia, where the base amount of the auction of the contract for the public house of prostitution was around thirty florins in the middle of the fifteenth century, the prostitutes paid thirty cents (a little less than five florins per year) to the manager for the monthly rent on the room in which they lived, on balance a modest expense and a cost of management probably not too high if we compare it to other data from the same region. For example, in May 1427 in Pisa[26] the office of the Consuls of the Sea rented the "small castle" to Simone di Migliore, for a total of three years, at a price of 800 florins per year, authorizing him to exact from the prostitutes thirteen cents a day, except Saturdays, when their activity was reduced and forbidden in several places, and when the price would be seven cents. But at the end of September the following year, after the many complaints and direct observation of the state of affairs, the same magistrates had to admit that the prostitutes were refusing to stay in that bordello, frightened as they were by such a "heavy" cost. Those who had stayed were indentured in perpetuity to the man, almost completely deprived of freedom, and reduced to being his slaves. With an act of "good government," the brothel keeper's commission was revoked and assigned to the ministers of the *Gabelle* of Pisa (Tax Office), a public entity that directly looked after and oversaw the premises and residences of the prostitutes as well as the maintenance of the building, collecting, in addition, the sum of four cents a day in rents,[27] a price still higher than what was paid in Pistoia but reduced with respect to what was exacted previously by the private leaseholder.

In the city of Florence, the costs of managing the public bordellos were varied and depended directly upon the size and quality of the buildings. The intermediaries rented from private citizens diverse types of residences, from a hotel to workshop-studios to small houses, all located in the space recognized and identified for the public exercise of prostitution, and then they, in turn, sublet to the women these premises in which to reside and work, paying to the municipality the required taxes. The hotel of Frascato, "where the prostitutes stay," with the addition of three "small workshops" in the street of chiasso Malacucina, was owned by Bernardo de' Medici who rented it to a certain Coppino for the sum of 117 florins per year. This Flemish man had already leased from the Pecori family a "small house with two exits to be used by hospitable women" for a price of twelve florins, all together considerable expenses. Bernardo de Medici, for his part, stated that he was unable in any way to exact the money and that he had decided not to "trouble himself" by reporting Coppino "because this is not the way of God."[28] At a later date, however, Coppino fled and, on top of that, robbed de' Medici of the furnishings of the house.[29] It was not only the great Florentine families who were involved in the real estate affairs of prostitution. Even the common people at times discovered that it could be profitable to rent out premises that they owned to people active in this business. This involvement is especially confirmed in the case of dwellings or workshop-studios that prostitution completely encompassed, precluding any possibility of leasing them to ordinary people.

Direct management by the municipalities guaranteed better prices and a certain autonomy for the women. It also gave them the added security of not falling into a spiral of debt that would leave them bound to private lease holders, paying sanctions, or incurring cautionary punishments for attempting to escape entrapment or failing to pay the required sums in their entirety. But perhaps this was not the most common form of management, and often, after brief periods during which the government intervened in cases of exploitation, municipalities reverted to the easier method of indirect management. The control over the running of the business became regulated and entrusted to judiciaries and officials in charge of it. These people, who in general established the costs and methods of collection, would also have had to monitor the situation so as to keep the women free from bullying and unjust demands for money.

9

A Disciplined Life

Is it possible to buy and sell a woman? In medieval societies, it was, and not only women but also men and children. Such purchases, however, were only legitimate with regard to slaves, bought in the market square and destined for domestic, artisanal, or agricultural labour, with the negotiating done legally and openly between authorized merchants and legitimate purchasers and, in the west, only on the condition that the slaves for sale had not been baptized and were not of the Christian faith. But in the sex trade everything is possible, and the fact that the purchase of women in such cases was not legal did not constitute a hindrance. The price of a woman did not concern only the temporary "purchase" or more precisely "loan" of her body, that is to say the tariff for her sexual favours. It also concerned the concept in its entire complexity – the price paid for the whole of her person, equal to that of a slave, with the difference that, generally speaking, slaves were much more valued.

What could have forced a woman into public prostitution in the brothels? And how did it happen that a free woman could become the object of an economic transaction, that she could get passed from hand to hand like a piece of property, indeed with the right to use her for special sexual favours? The fragmentary and extremely inadequate information we have does not entirely reveal the process. What we have does not tell us about the state of subservience that the woman had to be experiencing for her to be forced to accept or suffer a similar injustice. Perhaps it was a husband who claimed legal rights over her and whom she was incapable of resisting, out of weakness, or lack of resources and family support. Perhaps it was a lover, initially kind and persuasive, who had subsequently turned into a persecutor. Perhaps it was impotence and fragility that prevented her from reacting against a man, whatever his position, whatever his bond with her or his rights over her. Perhaps it was an act of sexual violence that transformed the victim, by now socially degraded and scorned, into an object at the mercy of her persecutor.

In July 1488, three florins were paid for a girl called Sandra about whose origins or circumstances we know nothing; we have just her name and the term *fanciulla* (girl or maiden) that defines her and leads us to believe that she was very young. Once the transaction was completed, Sandra was immediately brought to the Florentine brothel and kept there to earn her keep and pay back the amount of money her buyer, Bernardino Fede, had disbursed for her in order to reap profit from her body.[1] That was about the equivalent of the cost of a donkey in good condition, whose value fluctuated between one and four florins in the same time period depending on the age and constitution of the animal, but very far from the price of a good, young, and strong female slave whose price on the Florentine market went from forty-five to sixty florins. The price was only ever lower due to some serious physical malformation or bad character that might presage unpleasant behaviour. A few years earlier, on the same Florentine square, a pimp from Piedmont had acquired, from a Spanish cohort, an adolescent that came from Ferrara, a girl who might have been between twelve and thirteen years of age, for an even lower price: two florins and two pennies,[2] even though younger aged girls were usually esteemed as more valuable merchandise. The passage from hand to hand between the two pimps – and there is no indication in the document of any participation, consensus or even knowledge of the agreement on the part of the young girl – was obviously a common mode of exchanging protection over and income from a prostitute, who thus would see a change not in the chain around her neck but only in who was holding up her head. It seems difficult to imagine, however, that an adolescent of that age would have already been forced into the profession of prostitute and would already be beholden to a protector.

At the beginning of the century, in 1417, a young woman, recently married, avoided this fate, at least on one occasion, completely by chance. Her husband had, in fact, tried to sell her to the brothel keeper of Lucca but could not come to an agreement. The price he asked was too high – thirty florins – and the brothel keeper's offer too low – twelve florins to a maximum of sixteen – considering that she was so poorly dressed as to require a new wardrobe. On that day, Stella escaped the bordello, but future reconsideration on the part of the husband seems unlikely once the plan had been conceived and the first attempts in that direction made. Perhaps he may have lowered his demands or decided to invest a certain amount towards "dressing her anew" as he aspired towards future earnings.[3]

In whatever way women came to participate in the microcosm of organized prostitution, once they officially became public women they would have had to adapt to the regulations that governed that world, as in any community isolated from the rest of the collective, and live according to a special statute and to different and specific conventions and customs. Their daily life was defined by rules, obligations, and prohibitions. Their relationships with others, the protagonists of this world unto itself as represented by the bordello, the keepers, the pimps, and the clients, were measured in terms of the business and defined in a very specific way without taking into account human relationships. From the beginning of her life as a prostitute the woman had to complete the steps already codified for her. There existed some procedures of admission, to which she had to submit, and established principles to be respected. The first step brought her to register at the civic offices with specific jurisdiction in these matters, where she had to state generalities, like her origin, and whether there was a pimp accompanying her. She would leave the headquarters of the office armed with a licence and entrusted to a keeper who would choose the best location for her, inform her of her duties, and define the agreement to which she was subject.

Schedules, feast days, required days of abstinence, and prohibitions were meticulously outlined. The days were organized and always the same, the time to rest prescribed according to a calendar respectful of religious holidays, which in the Middle Ages were numerous in comparison with today, and during which they were, at times, forced to carry out rites of penitence. Permits to exit the premises were subject to certain conditions. Their obligations were precisely defined. Prices were decided upon by ordinances of the municipality, in terms of minimum tariffs, and by the keepers for the quality and quantity of sexual favours granted. Everyone, starting with those at the top – namely the managers – was required to observe the laws.

The code of laws, carefully and judiciously formulated, represented a theoretical summation that was most often disregarded, circumvented, and ignored. These regulations frequently give us a glimpse of a reality that did not correspond to norms. In some cities, twenty-year-old girls were not permitted into the bordellos, and yet the presence of extremely young girls, almost children, was frequent. Women who resided in the civic community were also not allowed to enter the brothels and participate there among the group of public women, but this prohibition was not always observed. The categorical ban on welcoming pregnant women was evaded on the pretext of ignorance or because the woman did not declare her state or because it was not obvious. But these practices existed – regularly in the case of pregnant women – although forbidden and sanctioned by the authorities. Money was even granted or lent for the woman's body, in such a way as to invest in it, pending its availability for sexual exploitation once the birth had taken place.

Although regulations differed from one city to another, some constants can be highlighted. Regarding admission into the brothels, for instance, in most of Castile the keepers could not accept women unless they were first examined by a doctor or a surgeon, who had to adequately minister to them if sick. However, sick women were wary of staying in the brothel, for fear of the spread of contagion, and were obliged to be transferred to hospital. In Valencia, acceptance into the bordello occurred in front of the office of Criminal Justice, which saw not only to the granting of licences to prostitutes but also to the entrusting of the woman to a keeper. A formal commitment to watch over her, especially in the case of illness, along with a guarantee of her good conduct was demanded of him. Daily needs were met by the brothel manager. In fact, the prostitutes had to rent their beds, linens, and blankets from him and, in addition, had to pay for food and drink. In exchange, he collected a part of their earnings, proportionately fixed by the authorities.[4] But these arrangements varied depending on the country, city, and agreement imposed by the managers who, despite laws and controls, often acted in such a way as to profit most without allowing the women any space to evade them or any margin of contractual power.

The work schedule, in general, began with the ringing of a bell in early morning and continued until the early night hours. During nocturnal hours, with a ban on moving around the city except for those with special safe conduct passes, no one could get into the brothel, but if one had already entered, staying inside the brothel was not forbidden even if the door was locked at the official closing time. Saturday, Sunday, and all Christian holidays were observed as days of rest, and prostitutes found working were punished. They were not allowed to exercise their profession outside of the brothel unless they had authorization from their overseer. Another responsibility of these latter individuals was to make absolutely sure that in the places under their authority no priests, monks, married men, Jews, or Muslims ever entered.

It was almost always forbidden to go out, except on predetermined days and then only wearing the designated symbols, or to eat elsewhere or to frequent the taverns. So it was established in 1367 in Barcelona by the city council. The municipality of Valencia also took this decision, and once it did, in 1350, women practitioners of prostitution were required to install themselves in the bordello, and they could not leave without permission. There was no choice. It was not an invitation that they could reject. Once their lifestyle and function were professed, they could only perform their duty in that place, under the control of the competent authorities, upon whom it was incumbent to decide what kind of clothes the women could wear on which occasions and when they could cross the threshold of the outer door of the brothel. They could not wear anything that might cause them to be mistaken for a decent woman: no cloak, no ornament, and on their shoulders a short yellow mantilla (scarf covering head and shoulders) of recognition.

According to Valencian regulations, it was forbidden for public prostitutes to work, and therefore to earn money, as they normally did, on Sundays, on other holidays, during Lent and the Ember days, and on New Year's Eve. The door of the *mancevia* (brothel) had to stay closed, and prostitutes who were discovered in violation of this rule were condemned to a punishment of one hundred lashes. Moreover, they were forbidden to sleep outside the brothel with men, which would make them seem to be women of greater quality and not public women, in order to obtain a higher price. In Spanish bordellos the keepers were called "father" and "mother," grotesque and false nicknames that feigned a type of family community though there was nothing paternal or maternal in their relationships with the prostitutes that they accommodated.

In Milan, Pavia, Venice, Turin, and other cities of Italy, the public women were compelled to live exclusively within the brothels and not to leave except on specific days, wearing the expected identifying symbol. In Venice, it was a yellow hanky around the neck, in Milan and Pavia, a hood and short shawl of white fustian that was buttoned in order to cover shoulders and breasts. In Turin, it was a tall and horned head covering, to which was added, in 1456 after an intense campaign of sermonizing, a yellow piece of string on the sleeve.[5] In Florence, on the other hand, during the course of the fifteenth century, registered and catalogued public women, whose activity took place in the house-brothel district, were exonerated from wearing these signs of infamy, but they came back into effect at the beginning of the sixteenth century.[6]In Perugia, a series of legislative measures from 1359, and then in 1398 and again in 1436, obliged the prostitutes to "go and stay in that prescribed public place of the bordello" called the bordello of *Malacucina*. They were forbidden to leave it for any reason whatsoever. Only on Saturday, when work was suspended, could they get permission to vacate the house, but only so long as they wore the compulsory strip of red material, three fingers long and one wide, sewn onto the right shoulder of their garment. At the start of the fifteenth century, the rules of obligatory residence in the bordello were reaffirmed with an intensification of penalties: a twenty lire fine for the first transgression, fifty for the second, and a flogging through the streets of the city for the third. The brothel keeper, to whom the woman "lent" her body, as it was so meaningfully and precisely set down in the Perugia regulations, was the one who presided over the person of the prostitute, through the loan of money, and the management of the business. He could beat her without incurring any penalty, provided that he did not hurt her so severely as to disable or kill her. He could have her imprisoned for debts, as long as these were witnessed by notarial deed or by a "pledge" written in the hand of a merchant, wool merchant, money changer or broker, or an apothecary at the headquarters of one of these guilds or in the presence of two witnesses. The prostitute would not be set free except upon receipt of payment and with the consent of her overseer.[7] The latter also made decisions with regard to possible expulsion. Difficult, quarrelsome, and obstinate women were sometimes thrown out in order to reinstate tranquillity in the brothels where internal peace had been disturbed. Maria de Osorio, Maria Nunnes, and Catalina the Turk, for example, were forced to leave the bordello in which they were residing because their conduct was judged to be scandalous and because some men died due to their behaviour. This happened in Murcia in the year 1476. The three women ended up prostituting themselves on the street.[8] Pimps in general did not have the same prerogatives. Their power was much more circumscribed, and they made use of their personal bond, and sometimes of a specific agreement settled verbally or by means of a written paper, to exercise some form of control over a woman. Provided the pimp possessed the necessary capital to do so, the surest method of control, as we will see, was to take charge of her debts.

Some late measures obliging prostitutes to stay and work only within the brothels prove to us that the prostitutes never stopped trying to avoid the brothel restrictions. In Murcia, in 1475, a municipal ordinance again forced some "malas mujeres cantoneras" (immoral streetwalkers), who were earning a living in an immoral and shameful way according to the city, to join the *puteria* (brothel) and stay there.[9] And again in the late fifteenth century in Ferrara, a ducal proclamation was issued on 21 August 1477 reminding "immoral" women to abandon the houses in which they conducted themselves scandalously and enter the bordello within three days or leave the city: "unde la mazore parte intròno in nave e sono andate ad altre citade, castelle e ville, unde la citade se hè nectar" ("hence most of them shipped off and went to other cities, castles, and villas, hence the city was cleansed"), reports the chronicler Bernardino Zambotti.[10]

Within the State of the House of Este, prostitutes had to present themselves at the Permit Office in order to obtain the right to reside in the capital as well as in the public bordello. It was at that office that they declared the general facts about themselves and paid entry taxes. Only after having completed these formalities did they acquire the right of access. They had to go through the same ritual upon leaving the city and pay a second tax. The prostitutes also had to explicitly state before this supervisory body if they were dependent on someone – namely whether they had one or more pimps – thus immediately disclosing their relationships. But the entire mechanism of control, of the collection of taxes, and the registration of the women, the pimps, and the relationships established between them, woefully began to collapse when the prostitutes secretly entered the city and just as furtively exited, ignoring every regulation, and evading the scrutiny of the authorities.[11]

In Florence, registration of every public woman took place at the Office of Onestá (the Office of Decency). The magisterial notary set down the name, origin, relationship of dependence with a protector (if such existed), and the placement assigned to her in a special book, and from that moment she was officially registered and subject to the control and authority of the officials. If the women wanted to declare a bond of reciprocal loyalty, and specific and stipulated agreements with a man, they were at liberty to do so. A note concerning this would be recorded for future reference and for their security. Following this, the only thing left to do was to try to integrate into the business and daily life of the neighbourhood. Truchin came from Flanders when she landed in the Tuscan city. She may have already lived elsewhere in Italian brothels and so may not have arrived directly from Flanders. It was the end of September 1436 when she presented herself before the Office of Decency in a dark alleyway flanked by tall palaces and received her assignment in a studio of the public brothel. She was also entrusted and supplied with a “small mattress” for which she was personally responsible. She was however refused a key with which to lock the door of her “workshop-studio.” And anyway, of what good would the key be, seeing as she, her body, her time, and her will were at the disposal of everyone?[12]

PART FOUR

The Business Itself

10

The Work, the People, the Debts

Despite monitoring by authorities, the will to regulate, and the organizational efforts of governments, we do not have enough specific documentation – encompassing and systematic – about this shadowy world to provide us with a profile and history beyond the barely discernible. We do not really know how many public women there were, what brought them to the bordello, who frequented them and derived pleasure from their bodies, and how many people lived off their backs. We do not possess significant and consistent data nor do we have complete narratives. We have to infer, hypothesize, and extend the little we do know into some sort of representation of reality. For example, we can infer that the bordellos were almost always inhabited by a foreign population, not necessarily from other countries but alien to the community, perhaps originating from cities and regions that were close by but sometimes from very far away, from places that were geographically, politically, linguistically, and culturally different. This would result in a permanent type of estrangement because these people did not stay long enough in one place to make it home. They continually returned to the road, thus constituting an itinerant microcosm that ended up finding and living in places that had, at any rate, many similarities. German, Spanish, French, and Italian bordellos had their own characteristics, structure, mother tongue, and cuisine, but many languages were spoken in each. One met fellow countrymen or fellow citizens there. The same gestures were performed in all of them, and the walls were what they were: stone fences.

In Valencia, over a thirty-year period, a total of 676 women were recorded as having broken the law. Only in 12.27 per cent of those cases was the place of origin of the women indicated: of eighty-three prostitutes who broke the law, forty-four came from various cities in Castile – Cordoba, Burgos, Seville, Murcia, and Toledo among others. The war that had ravaged the communities of the kingdom had likely contributed to their abandonment of those places. Six of the prostitutes came from the kingdom of Aragon, four from Navarre, two from Catalonia, two from Majorca, eight from Italy, six from France, three from Portugal, two from Greece, and six were residents of Valencia.[1] This is very little through which to identify flows of traffic. We must not forget, as well, that sometimes the definitions of countries of origin were imprecise in terms of geography, though rather suggestive when they employed an evocative long lost nickname for a place or a region, perhaps belonging only to the nostalgically remembered distant land of a woman's family, or originating from an important and insistent biographical detail in her memory.

The residual Florentine documentation allows us a glimpse of a cosmopolitan environment within the prostitution zone. Many of the women living there, and the men who associated with them, came from outside the Florentine state and from countries beyond the current borders of Italy. And yet it is necessary to highlight the imprecision and frequently the generic nature of the attribution of place. For instance, a German of the fifteenth century was part of a linguistic and cultural community that extended from Bruges to Krakow, and, therefore, a Brabantian or Flemish person could be hidden, according to this definition, among the people of Alamannia or Alamannia alta or of the Magna, while the word "Slav" identified both Poles and Slavs from the south, also called "Slavonians," a term that, at the same time, defined the inhabitants of the Dalmatian coast, directly annexed to the rule of

Venice. The geographic denominations of that time, moreover, do not correspond to present territorial allocations. In 1436 when the Office of Decency carried out a census, seventy-one prostitutes and twenty-eight pimps populated the bordello district. Most of the women came from the Netherlands, followed by Germans, northern Italians (almost all of whom were Venetian), and finally French and Slavonians. A Spanish woman, an Irish woman, a Swiss, a Greek, and a Florentine were single representatives of their own lands. As far as the men are concerned, first place went to northern Italians, followed by Flemish and then Germans. During the course of the century this flow of immigration tied to prostitution began to show different characteristics, maintaining, however, the predominance of the ethnic-linguistic groups already observed. There were sporadic arrivals of women from the south of Italy, Sardinia, and Corsica in the decade of 1441–51 and, in the next decade, of Slavic women from the north while, in addition to those already pointed out, there was the isolated presence of a Hungarian and a "gypsy," and two Circassians were also observed. But true change manifested itself clearly at the end of the century when, from among around eighty prostitutes, the absolute majority was represented by northern Italians, followed by a minority of Spaniards, Flemish women, and Greeks. A small number were Germans, French, southern Slavs, and southern Italians. The male staff at that time was totally composed of men hailing from northern Italy.

The evolution of the brothel population in terms of the presence of foreign or imported people follows a different curve in the city of Ferrara. In 1438, Italian prostitutes from Lombardy and the Veneto were in the majority. Then came the Emilians not from Ferrara. A few were from beyond the Alps, first among whom were Germans. Nine of the fourteen identifiable pimps came from the Netherlands, Flanders, and Brabant. Three were German, and two from the Veneto area, specifically Treviso and Verona. Two managers of the hotel-brothels were from Ferrara. One was from Bologna, and one from Bergamo. In the second half of the fifteenth century, data reveals that the prostitutes were mostly German and Venetian, then Slav; very few were from Lombardy or the Netherlands, with an inversion of this tendency with respect to the Florentine reality. In the case of Ferrara, the majority of the men involved were northern Italians, followed by some Germans and Tuscans.[2]

In Palermo, public women came, above all, from regions of today's Spain. Judging by the nicknames or identification by means of place of origin, many women arrived in the Sicilian city from Perpignan, Toledo, and, in general, more came from Castile or Aragon.[3]

How can we explain these migration flows? What is the significance of these specific starting points? What could be the reason for these transitions or fluxes over the years? And what mindset compelled these men and women to set off and "travel the earth." Was Florence or Pisa, Valencia or Dijon or Ulm, Arles or Paris or London the goal that they had in mind and which they tried to reach right from the beginning? Unfortunately there is no evidence enabling us to reconstruct their journeys, motivations, or expectations nor of providing any knowledge of the places they passed through or of the path news travelled. An oppressive silence reigns over these lives. If we wish to ponder a moment longer, we must proceed indirectly and attempt to evaluate, on one side, the powers of attraction of the most important European cities and, on the other, the powers of adversity and misfortune linked to the geographical, economic, and political characteristics of the realities abandoned. And this, broadly speaking, can apply to other places and nationalities. None of these considerations, however, can replace the riches of a personal narration. Each individual story contains episodes and motives that differentiate it from others. And this is something we cannot recreate.

The capital of the Florentine state, like Milan, Venice, Naples, Paris, or London, just to mention a few of the more dynamic cities of the era, had excellent opportunities attractive to foreigners. Merchants and travellers had made these places internationally famous. The manufacturing economy, in the textile sectors of wool and silk, in tapestry weaving, in arms manufacture, in the art of gold and jewellery handicraft, and in creating monumental works, continuously attracted foreign labourers, and a specialized workforce, who ended up settling down and building a resident and stable community of Flemish, German, and various types of Italian immigrants. Domestic servants and labourers flowed in from Eastern Europe, the Balkans, and the coast of Dalmatia. The presence of immigrants in itself constituted a magnet for itinerant prostitutes and pimps. Perhaps the possibility of hearing a familiar language and of finding clients among the numerous single and lonely males in a foreign land at times motivated the choice of a large, populous, and industrious urban centre.[4] Almost every European city had its small or large percentage of immigrant foreigners – a reservoir of manpower – integrating into the labour market, either continuously or intermittently. But sometimes, prostitutes and pimps could emerge out of the ranks of immigrants, either waiting to be employed, or having been employed then ousted from the workforce. If at the beginning the voyage had been long, it became extremely short in the city, as one moved from district to district, possibly the distance of only a few streets. Ultimately a worker might abandon the world of manufacturing, and, with a life partner in tow, enter the world of the bordello.

Furthermore, there were places in which environmental, climactic, economic, and political factors generated a chronic exodus of people and irreversibly instigated migrations. Various regions of Corsica, Albania, and of the Carpathians were traditionally among these. Economic conditions, wars, epidemics, and tax increases occasionally provoked the exile of men and women even from lands not usually classified as those from which people emigrated, such as France or Flanders, which during the long Anglo-French conflict, known as the Hundred Years' War, sent many in flight from the forces of destruction.[5]

Some couples of prostitute and pimp arrived fully formed and presented themselves for registration as an established partnership, declaring their bond and availability to continue their "work," initiated elsewhere, in the new location. They usually came from the same geographic-linguistic area, but since they probably had not directly arrived from their places of origin, those disclosed to the officials, it was thus possible that theirs was a recent encounter, a newly minted agreement, established before setting off from their last port of call. At any rate, these unions were not initiated out of passion, affection, or love, at least not always, although we cannot exclude this possibility, but rather out of convenience. Sometimes, for the woman, they might represent an undesirable obligation born out of a promise of protection, and less oppression on the part of the man, and out of an expectation of good income and better profits for both. If the prostitute was particularly attractive and expert, or the pimp less greedy, the partnership might have developed because of a circumstance of dependency, if debts shackled the woman and she no longer had anything upon which to live and with which to pay her creditors. Someone who could lift her from under the oppressive weight of debt, by buying the amount owed, momentarily resembled a benefactor and not the prison guard that he would certainly become with time.

The cost of the prostitutes' exercise of their profession, even where it was not that high or where it was reduced after protests and entreaties, always represented amounts exceeding their earnings. Taxes, rent on their rooms, the cost of food, percentages paid to the brothel keepers and the maintenance of pimps, the cost of cosmetics, ornaments, and clothes, which on first entering the bordello might seem manageable or even minor, certainly not worrisome – amounts to be paid in a nebulous future – ended up weighing heavily, as soon as the women began to accumulate creditors making demands upon them. A sickness, holidays, days of forced abstention from work, a slowdown in business for various reasons, possible fines for rule infractions all worsened the situation and made precarious any recovery of money that would have lightened the debt load. The pursuit of money became exhausting. Creditors were never understanding or obliging. In the case of some prostitutes, creditors could become aggressive and violent and insist on payment in many forms. The keepers had the right to imprison the prostitutes under their management. Their protectors felt justified in hitting and hurting them, even with weapons. Suppliers, acquaintances, and clients claimed their due before the law. The chances of a way out were slim. With this anxiety over acquiring money to pay their creditors, the women would ask for the loan of other monies, thus accumulating a new debt in the illusion that this would take care of something, partially fill the bottomless pit, and that postponement would do the rest. They could pawn a dress, sell a necklace, or steal without succeeding in getting out from under the burden of debt. We can understand the relief of finding someone who would buy off their debts entirely, even though that meant a slave-like relationship and complete loss of autonomy, freedom, and financial potential. In such a case, the prostitute's body might no longer be for sale as before, because someone had bought it completely and was profiting from it, granting her merely the right to feed herself, in order to survive, to dress, to exhibit herself, and to satisfy one man in order to enrich another.

Some of the expenses that a prostitute had to sustain have already been partially identified. The right to be admitted into the city, for example, or to be accepted and "protected" within a bordello was taxed. On the Iberian Peninsula the tax was called a *perdiz*. In Italy it was called a *gabella*, and in France a *gabelle*. Generally speaking, it was paid to the appropriate officials and varied with regard to quantity: it was practically symbolic in London, modest in Dijon, burdensome in Toulouse.[6] In Milan, prostitutes even had to shoulder the salary – amounting to two cents each – of the official responsible for the closing of the brothel door to prevent access during the night hours.[7] In Pistoia, as has already been said, a prostitute spent thirty cents a month on the rent of her room in addition to a certain amount (we don't know how much) of money for "bread and wine," in other words for her food. In Pisa, the daily price of the rent had been established at thirteen cents before it was reduced to seven by public officials, and in Florence the monthly rate varied between ten and thirteen lire (equal to or more than 200 cents). Facts and figures are not really representative, considering their scarce and fragmentary nature. Often they are not comparable because we do not know the terms of the different contracts represented – if, for instance, food or taxes were included or, alternatively, if the amounts only covered the lease for the premises. Furthermore, the brothel keeper reserved the right to keep up to a third of the woman's earnings towards the cost of her maintenance. To evaluate what that was we can consider data from Toulouse where in 1514 the keepers declared that they had spent one cent and three deniers per day or data from Dijon two years later where it was the exact double of that amount: two cents and six deniers.[8]

But the signed contracts between these keepers and the prostitutes, just as in the case of work conditions, varied enormously. In the brothel of the city of Perugia, for example, in 1388 Isabetta, a public prostitute from Bologna, voluntarily engaged herself to Ranaldo di Nicolò, called Boccaccio, who was from the Perugia neighbourhood of Porta Sole, and the brothel keeper. Isabetta agreed "servire et famulari in loco postribuli more meretricali" (to serve as a prostitute in the brothel) for two years beginning on 1 August without any salary or compensation and promised to hand over all of her earnings to the man. In exchange, she received thirty florins in "pannis et vestimentis et certis laboreriis argenti" (clothes, dresses, and silver objects). Ranaldo also undertook to "vestire, alimentare et gubernare competenter secundum condecentiam sue persone" (clothe, feed, and competently govern the woman as befits her person).[9] Since a substantial financial fine was often imposed on the women who didn't keep their promises, the agreement seems to be a form of economic slavery. The prostitutes were in fact deprived of direct revenues, albeit temporarily, and depended for their food, clothes, and any other necessity on the generosity of the keeper, who would discreetly exercise that generosity according to the "quality" (rather low being a prostitute) of the person to whom it was directed, as it was carefully highlighted in the formal agreements. No one, lawmaker or private citizen, ever sought to discuss the "disgraceful" circumstances of a prostitute, therefore it makes us think that Ranaldo felt free not to come across as too munificent with her. Those florins, which, on the spot, seemed like so much money to hold in one's hands, represented the only money the woman would have for a long time, and with which she could face many unforeseen events. But it is necessary to underscore the terms of payment of the negotiated florins, chosen by the man for this type of servitude, paid not in cash but in generic moveable goods, listed vaguely in the document, which testifies to the man's shrewdness. In a normal deed, if the choice was to pay in clothes and ornaments, a notary or public official would have had to draw up a precise inventory, containing an appraisal and the corresponding monetary value. In this way, based on promises always so indefinite, the life of the prostitute was cast aside.

On the same day, and according to similar stipulations, the astute keeper advantageously secured for himself two other women. Vannina from Florence received twenty-three florins but had to commit to working one year for him and the promise to pay back fifty florins if she left before the year ended. Iacopa from Siena committed herself to the same conditions. In the autumn of that year, 14 November, to be exact, even more favourable agreements were negotiated with anoth er woman from Siena named Caterina. For twenty-five florins, this time paid in cash, she undertook to work for two years, giving up her entire income, while the man promised to "eam vestire, calzare, alimentare et gubernare secundum qualitatem sue persone"[10] (dress her, provide her with shoes, feed her, and govern her according to the quality of her person). Giovanna from Catania received thirty florins, but her contract was for three years, and she also had to hand over to Ranaldo all of her income from sexual favours. The differences in treatment depended on the plight and neediness of the prostitute, as well as on her contractual abilities. An indebted woman, without resources and perhaps not that attractive was less likely to come to an agreement that was favourable to her. On the other hand, the young and promising prostitute, who had been managing her body to her benefit, could have negotiated more profitable terms.

With such variability in contractual conditions, in the amounts of the taxes, and in the expenses that the prostitute had to sustain, it is almost impossible to extract data of significance and be able to compare and contrast it. Throughout the fifteenth century, in central Italy, a day of nonspecialized manual labour could be remunerated with the sum of ten cents. For the sake of comparison, this amount would have made it difficult to even procure a room for rent in a bordello. Unfortunately the most important elements of comparison are missing – the overall income a prostitute was able to earn in one day or the income from each sexual encounter. The scarcity of information authorizes us to only make hypotheses in terms of scale. According to Jacques Rossiaud the minimum tariff in the bordellos, established by the keepers but especially monitored by the governors through repeated ordinances, equalled a quarter, a sixth, or an eighth of the daily salary of a day labourer or an artisan. This was also true of southern Germany, Castile, the kingdom of Valencia, Andalusia, Italy and Burgundy.[11] In Nuremberg, a day labourer earning eight to nine pfennigs a day could afford three to four visits to the bordello, while an artisan earning sixteen to twenty pfennigs could afford at least six to eight visits unless he intended to spend the whole night with a woman because that would cost three to four times more. Comparing the work of a prostitute to that of a salaried field hand, she would have to dispense two sexual services to equal an entire day of work in a vineyard.

Comparisons, however, have very limited value: no worker could afford to squander the income from his strenuous and uncertain labour on some brief fling in the arms of a prostitute, given that he had to provide for himself, often for a family, and take into account the limited continuity of paid days in the course of a year. Of course it could be said that the cost was not prohibitive for the salaried classes, who were after all the most prevalent consumers of public brothels. In terms of everyday life, barring exceptions, the public bordello seemed illsuited to the rich bourgeois and aristocrats, who had full recourse to the reserves of domestic slaves and servants of whom they took advantage at home.

And yet, beyond the scarcity of uncertain data, one well documented and significant phenomenon of the life circumstances of these women can be confirmed: their chronic state of indebtedness about which we have already hinted. Many prostitutes possessed nothing, not even what they wore, and were not able to put aside any money or, often, pay what they owed to the state and to those who provided lodging and board.[12] A Brabantian public prostitute in Florence, on the street of chiasso dei Buoi, had accumulated a debt of fourteen florins to her keeper. In order to maintain the cost of her rent and food, she reached an agreement with her keeper. It called for payment in thirteen instalments,[13] but a peaceful settlement was not on the agenda, and the amounts due were too high to allow for a rapid end to her outstanding unpaid bills. Frequently the keepers would then request the incarceration of the debtors for a few days or weeks with the intention of compelling these insolvent women to find a solution. It is difficult to believe that they could all of a sudden find the money that had been unavailable to them beforehand, but this kind of blackmail was useful in making them even more committed, by forcing them to work more, or in depriving them of some dress or necklace, by pawning those articles. Besides this, the power of the managers to request jail time and then grant release "out of clemency and love" also constituted a means of punishing women who were rebellious and antagonistic towards the discipline of the brothel.[14]

The holders of brothel leases were generally the prostitutes' most significant creditors, given that they were the primary providers of goods and services and that they claimed a percentage of the prostitutes' earnings, if not the entirety of those amounts. In 1427, Betto di Zanobi, the keeper of the Macciana hotel-brothel in Florence declared that he had to collect 127 florins from twelve women lodging in his premises. The lowest individual debt was three florins, the highest twenty-four. If the cost for annual maintenance of a person in that period was calculated at fourteen florins, one can easily deduce the magnitude of the debenture. This is not an isolated case: in 1429 Leone di Arigo, a Flemish keeper, when drawing up his last will and testament on his deathbed, left, *amore Dei* (for love of God), the sum of six florins to three prostitutes who were also Flemish and residents of his brothel, an amount to deduct from the debt that they had incurred with him. Since the term deduct is used, we can presume that this sum did not completely dispose of the amount owed.[15]

Where the brothel managers are concerned, a prostitute's inability to repay a debt resulted in the creation of a relationship of personal dependency: the woman lost her right to self-determination and often had to make a commitment to stay, for a period of time determined by her keeper, until the termination of her pledge. But there is some important evidence to consider in these contractual obligations and what stands out is a real economic system. The lack of means revealed in these transactions speaks of a lack of revenue. The women were hard pressed to maintain a respectable and satisfying standard of living through earnings from the sale of their bodies. In order to provide for a daily minimum, food and lodgings, they were often forced to request a loan, and most often this occurred for the purchase of superfluous goods. Taking out a loan with the brothel keeper, a pimp, or a client outside the ranks of the bordello placed the prostitute in a position of obligation that could not be deferred for very long. Prostitutes were known to be unreliable debtors. They did not take care to respect deadlines or payment of instalments. They were always ready to opt for escape, when they found themselves in a desperate situation with no way out, and chasing after them to prosecute them by law was lengthy, complex, and difficult.

So in order to procure the necessary money to eliminate their outstanding unpaid bills, or at least reduce the debt while waiting for better times, the prostitutes could resort to the expedient of pawning their finest and most expensive garments or some necklace. Sometimes, however, they found themselves, after a while, having to redeem these objects out of necessity, and, in order to do that, had to request another loan. A German woman, called Lisabetta, had pawned, out of necessity, an entire wardrobe made up of quite valuable clothing: two tunics, one of a turquoise shade with embroidery that enhanced a sleeve, the other designed with peach blossoms; three gamurras (a dress with a fitted bodice and a skirt worn over a chemise, either front-laced or side-laced), which were more elegant than simple tunics, two being green, one of which had a train, the other with crimson sleeves, and the third of a pinkish colour with velvet green sleeves. Besides these, she possessed a silver chain and a belt. The full value of her wardrobe was thirty-three florins. But once she got her wardrobe back, the goods belonged to her no more than before because, in advancing her the money, to which was added six florins to be paid to a carter, her keeper demanded the redeemed merchandise as a guarantee.[16]

Thus the chain of debts and insolvency was extended, the number of creditors expanded, and the owed sums passed from one person to another. Indeed, in a complicated process which represented a substantial part of the market economy in the area of sexual exploitation, the debts of prostitutes could be bought and removed by anyone: a different brothel keeper, a bordello client, even a person totally outside of that world, an artisan, for instance, who intended to establish himself in business. If we exclude rare and generous charitable interventions that would liberate the women from these burdens limiting their freedom, the act of acquiring a prostitute's liabilities allowed one to also acquire the right to use and exploit her. One paid a more or less elevated sum of money and received in response a means of producing income.

Besides the brothel managers, pimps, and clients, circling the prostitutes was a small crowd of otherwise random people – labourers and artisans, from rag and bone men to tailors, from grocers to barbers – who eventually came into contact with them. The purchase or loan of a piece of fabric, foodstuffs, the sewing of a dress, medical attention (when a prostitute could not afford a costly professional she had to settle for the ministrations of a barber) made these encounters possible and necessary. Perhaps some of them, besides being suppliers, belonged as well to the general clientele. Whatever the case, many of them, if not all, were interested in the state of neediness into which the public women were in the habit of falling. They were ready to take over the debts and to lend money. They were aware that by doing this they earned a great deal in the process, whether through collectible interest, unencumbered as they would be by any type of regulation in these circumstances, or through the acquisition of rights over the women in question in case of her failure to pay back the debt. The prostitutes thus became a business transaction, bound by financial hardship to those who became, at least temporarily, their masters through entitlement.

In Ferrara, the prostitutes' circumstances were no different than what was experienced in the Tuscan capital and many other European cities. They became bound "pro pane et vino" (for bread and wine), their lodgings, clothes, shoes, for some unexpected sickness and the related medications, to brothel keepers, innkeepers, pimps, and regular people who found an opportunity to exploit them. The story of Ursolina from Udine stands out from others, Germans or Italians. In 1482 she was forced to acknowledge a debt of three ducats to a certain Bartolo. Upon confessing her indebtedness, the woman revealed a chain of creditors of which Bartolo represented only the last and most recent link. She revealed that she was in arrears to a certain Francesco Cazavilano from Comacchio, who, in turn had bought her debt from Nardo of Reggio, the landlord at the brothel of Gambero. It is quite possible that through these transactions, the quantity owed changed and actually swelled by virtue of interest and waiting periods.[17] Debts represented a constant torment to prostitutes. They followed the women through their days and their relocations. Often they caused hasty departures from one city, but the debts were not in that way abandoned. They stayed by their side, sometimes embodied in the man who had purchased the debt, or were sometimes just steps behind – in the time it took for a complaint to arrive from the competent authority or the time it took for an official letter to reach them.

Caterina was a Slavonian from the Dalmatian Coast under the dominion of the Republic of Venice. That was where she settled and began to accumulate outstanding bills, one after another, all of which her man tried to settle, even though they were quite substantial. She owed one gold ducat to a Venetian bath manager, two ducats to pay for some coloured fabric that she had purchased from a "rag dealer," four ducats for food, and finally fifty cents for a month of board in the city. And yet, when she left Venice for Ferrara, Caterina had changed companions, and we find her with Pietro di Matteo from Treviso, who took over her protection, having bought her through the reimbursement of all outstanding monies to her excompanion and protector. In almost a year spent in the capital of the d'Este state, she continued to accumulate debts: two ducats and sixty-two cents for food and beverages consumed in the Gambero tavern, without ever having settled her previous ones.[18]

The imposing presence of a brothel keeper, looming over the freedom and life of the prostitutes did not preclude the simultaneous and towering profile of a pimp by their side. These two figures, inasmuch as they had separate and distinct functions, seem to overlap in this realm of exploitation. The capacity for pimps to earn a living was linked to the sale of the woman and her sexual favours, but in the case of lease-holding keepers, with some exceptions, the attachment was almost impersonal. He managed an enterprise and governed a group of subjects. The pimp, on the other hand, maintained a one-to-one relationship with the prostitute, one in which he had many rights and some sporadic duties, like that of protection, well compensated for by his being maintained in a life of idleness. If the pimp had more than one woman under his protection, then the relationships were of a different nature.

The phenomenon was so conspicuous and the privations so evident that many persons of a charitable temperament hint at this in fifteenth-century documents from Ferrara. These are people who actively tried to alleviate the prostitute's suffering and especially her personal dependence. Sometimes the charitable bequests were to be used in a generic way to "free the prostitutes from the brothels or more specifically a woman from an immoral overseer." In 1434, it was the Marquis Nicholas III who authorized the payment of fifty lire to a keeper, Giovanni from Constantinople, in order to wipe out the debts Giovanni held for six prostitutes. The declaration listed in a detailed way who were to be the receivers of this charity: "the 'violet' sinners in the common brothel" – Margherita from "Alemagna," Margherita from Ljubljana, Catelina from "Senalza," Margherita of "Slavonia,"Agnola of "Alemagna," and Catelina of Brabant. The purpose of this munificent gift was also indicated with transparent clarity. The debts incurred by these women were being paid so that they could "forget and free themselves of the place."[19] The marquis intended to liberate them, to return the dignity of free choice to them so that they could distance themselves from that specific place in order to start over elsewhere or change their lives, but it does not stipulate that they must stop prostituting themselves.

The prostitutes serviced a numerous and varied population – young and old, city and country dwellers, people of the area and foreigners – however, most of the clientele was represented by salaried workers, servants, modest artisans, peasants who were in the city to sell their produce at the market or to take care of a little business, soldiers, merchants, tradesmen, and perhaps a travelling foreigner of higher means and social position. Not all foreigners reported as users of the bordello were actually such. They may have belonged to the widespread communities of Germans, Flemish, Slavonians, and Lombards, just as Italians were often identified in a broader sense – people present in the major cities of Europe. Access to the public brothels was forbidden to married men, clerics, Jews, and Muslims, and the sanctions imposed for each infraction to the rule were so severe that they dissuaded keepers and prostitutes from making exceptions. If discovered, they pled ignorance: no one knew, imagined, or had been informed. But, whereas the prohibition against persons of the Jewish faith was generally respected, due to religious and social prejudice, the same conviction and effectiveness was not always exercised when prohibiting the entry of clergy and, especially, married men. French testimonies relating to the bordellos of Dijon and Lyons refer to clients as "good young men" propelled by their urges. "Nature pushes them to go and amuse themselves." "Nature moves them," is the explanation offered in some documents, almost as if their presence is justified as an uncontrollable command dictated by an unassailable force.[20]

The wealthier clients who frequented the "indecent places," though not frequently, would show up there on special occasions, particular celebrations, perhaps together with a group of friends. This did not exclude the private and personal use of the bordello. And often a woman, casually encountered within those walls, became a habitual lover to be brought into one's own home, in the city or onto one's country estates, with permission from the brothel keeper. This could become a habit, perpetuated in order to enjoy the services of a prostitute on one's own or with others in a more comfortable and private way and one which represented an excellent chance for the prostitute not only to earn more but also to establish a personal relationship with a rich client, harbinger of future advantages: gifts, support, and maybe even a future outside of the bordello.

11

Marked for Life

There is a desire in a whore to be not just mere meat. There is a kind of urgency, you might say, to be accepted as a human. And not ... just "a pound or two of dog's dinner done up pretty, a hole in the wall."

Nell Kimball, *Her Life as an American Madam*

It was Sunday, 28 February 1497. Girolamo Savonarola, a friar of the Dominican Order, had filled the square, as was his wont, when his presence and a sermon was announced. On that day, his heated words of disdain fell like burning embers on the corruption of Rome, an indecent spectacle of moral poverty, and frenziedly railed against prostitutes.

> Is there no one of them here in Italy and Rome? A thousand are few in Rome, ten thousand are few, twelve thousand are few, fourteen thousand are few in Rome. Listen then to these words, O cows of Samaria ... The cow is a stupid and fat animal and just like a piece of meat with eyes ... Could it be that you are not ashamed, that you are not only concubines, but concubines of priests and friars, and yet you do this publicly?[1]

He defined them as "fat cows" with all of the contempt for bodies of mere flesh, indeed, not even bodies, only pieces of meat, and incited his public and mostly respectable women to banish them from the streets where they gathered. Times had changed in relation to the beginning of the century when the plan had been to control and make available prostitution as a public service, deemed indispensible and redemptive, in an orderly, decorous, and disciplined manner. But now disorder had returned to the streets and bordellos, women had shown themselves to be undisciplined and desirous of fleeing the places expressly set up for them, and pimps and brothel keepers had revealed themselves to be, in many cases, much the same as unrepentant malefactors, and the political certainty of the ruling classes was beginning to waver. In Mantua, on two occasions, in 1491 and 1493, Isabella Gonzaga and Francesco II answered the call to order all prostitutes to register in the Scimmia public bordello and to stay and live there or else leave the city and the state.[2]

With the offensive coming from inspired and indefatigable preachers, who travelled the streets, going from city to city and from square to square, and then returned to threaten hell on earth, the governors also began to think over and redefine their enterprise of tolerance. They restored the signs where they had been abolished, reinforced them where they were not conspicuous enough, banned prostitutes and pimps from their territories, emptied the bordellos, and increased controls on clandestine prostitution. Sometimes they acted only on a wave of emotion inspired by the coming of a cleric of some fame, heralded by reports of the fear and suggestiveness of imminent catastrophe invoked in other cities he had visited. News of measures taken by other governments reached them along with these preachers, and thus an atmosphere of superstitious apprehension was transmitted. What would have happened if a similar approach had not been taken, if the state had not been vacated by sinners and corruptors? Would the plague really have come to devastate and sow death? In doubt, it seems the authorities thought it would be better to avoid the risk by acting as others had, with condemnations and bans. With the sermons' echoes fading after a sufficient lapse of time, the brothels became once again populated, the women returned to sell themselves, the pimps to gamble and drink and live off their backs, the keepers to exploit them all. With little commotion, things returned to normal, the emergency over. However, something had truly changed and in an irreversible way.

In many places, the public women were forced to continuously wear the symbols of their "art," without the process of legalization and their confinement within the bordellos exonerating them from wearing those symbols during their authorized departures. Besides the cloth strips or bands of yellow or red, the capes of white fustian, or the head coverings that immediately signalled who they were to the attention of everyone, other distinctions, prohibitions, and restrictions on clothing and footwear additionally served to distinguish them and mark them recognizable for what they were: women for public pleasure, women for collective consumption. In Foligno, in the middle of the sixteenth century, it was the bishop who ordered prostitutes, pimps, and other women who lived an "indecent, lascivious, and evil life" to adopt a new distinctive symbol – a turquoise veil thirty centimetres long and at least twenty wide worn on their heads above any other cloth, cap, or head covering. In Bologna, a law issued on 28 August 1566 forced the prostitutes, "as a sign of their shamelessness," to wear a shroud on their head and above it a "hat or cap with or without a feather." About a year later, the regulation was changed and compelled all prostitutes to wear a white cap of any fabric other than silk.[3] And where, as in Florence, prostitutes were freed of these shameful signs during the century of the good governance of prostitution, the failure of that political undertaking induced those responsible to go back to the old ways and restore the stigma of disparity, the symbol of impurity and social contempt.

But there were other signs that were more onerous, more indelible, since they were carved into one's flesh. We cannot speak about the invisible marks on one's dignity, life, self-esteem, unrealized dreams, unfulfilled desires, and frustrated aspirations because they remain indecipherable, unsaid, not transmitted, but the scars on the body have left their evidence. The bordellos, the districts of the prostitutes, the places dedicated to the pleasures of men were not islands of tranquility and wellbeing, at least not for the women deployed to work there. Apart from relations with clients – apart from the high probability that clients could become violent, could beat them and hurt them, or leave without paying – coexistence with their colleagues, their pimps and those of others and their keeper/masters, was not easy. And it certainly was not as idyllic as the law reformers had imagined. Rivalries, jealousies, antipathies, infighting, originating as well from the diverse nationalities, arose with some frequency between the prostitutes and found expression in verbal protests, insults, and even physical aggression. Their dependence on men, whatever role or position of those, kept the prostitutes constantly in a position of economic, physical, and legal subordination. Undoubtedly there were rebellions, gestures of hostility, or appeals to the legal protection of the institutions, but on the whole the women were more often victims than culprits. In documents from Valencia, regarding the public brothel, the prostitutes appear as protagonists in robberies and various injustices, but in turn, and indeed more frequently, they were the victims of violent acts: assaulted with blows and wounds from weapons by pimps, clients, and coworkers, with the aggressors in Valencia almost always men.[4]

As we have seen, the public women in almost all countries of Europe were subjected to special legislation and a specific jurisdiction, different from the regular one, to which they could not appeal even if they had wanted to. It could happen, therefore, that in a dispute with a client or with a person alien to the world of prostitution, the magistracy could judge its own subject (the prostitute) but would not be able to put on trial, much less condemn, the other party. The judgment risked being uneven because often the examination of the hostile party did not take place and because most often there existed a presumption of guilt with respect to the prostitute. She was guilty because she was of inferior status, guilty because she had infuriated, guilty because she was subjected to the protection of someone and had not taken this into account, guilty because outrage had been brought upon an honourable citizen. Even when admitting an element of guilt, the correspondent often slipped through the net of the law as he was either delivered to a different judiciary or not even accused. There was a substantial difference in how justice was meted out to the prostitutes. Consider Anna, who was punished for having hit a client. She was effectively guilty, having pursued him with a stick and having managed to hit him once on the head. However the man, previous to her attack and having consummated the act, had grabbed hold of his knife – though according to the law he was not allowed to be armed – and had pointed it at her and tried to leave without paying.[5] But the crime and the punishment that was handed down in judgment refer only to her. She had assaulted. She had struck. Although we cannot exclude the possibility that elsewhere, in another court and with another magistracy, the man was condemned, the fact that Anna had suffered an armed assault was not considered an extenuating circumstance in her case nor was it taken into account towards administering a lighter sentence.

What is more, public prostitutes were subject to the authority of the brothel keepers, who, according to the applicable regulations, had rights and powers over them, rights and powers they couldn't have had over any free person. They had the freedom to throw them out, to punish them, and even to do so physically. They were permitted to request imprisonment for them, as well as determine the length of their incarceration, which was imposed on the basis of individual will rather than established by law. Very often caused by indebtedness to the keeper himself, the prison sentences were lengthened or shortened depending on the abilities and resources of women to find a guarantor or a lender. But it was neither implausible nor rare that prison worked to calm rebellion, punish some sort of disobedience, tame the wild temperament of someone ill disposed towards subjugation, and to make it clear, to one and all, just who wielded the power. The sentence could be a few days, a few weeks, two months – a length of time that was variable and not predefined – to be lived in the uncertainty of what might happen, of how much longer detention in a place of inhospitable segregation might last, at the mercy of rough prison guards, perhaps capable of abuses, and in the worst conditions of daily life. And maybe a woman had to experience prison more than once: if she could not pay off her debt, find the strength to simply bow her head, or if she was not able to escape to anywhere else. Prison leaves scars. It inspires fear and makes you defenceless, especially if you are ignorant of the duration of the punishment, which for prostitutes was indefinite and unknowable. It could be long or short. Even for public women, used to being treated as a means, as objects, inured to being insulted, derided, humiliated, beaten, and assaulted, individuals who were also strong, returning blows and using language that was often lewd and improper, women who could be brazen – even for them – incarceration was a bitter pill. So, too, were the punishments in public, staged as entertainment, and functioning as a warning.

It was on a Friday, 21 August 1489, in Ferrara, in the central square smouldering in the heat, when the superintendent of the tax office, assigned to matters concerning prostitution, decided to teach two prostitutes a lesson because they were guilty of assaulting a peasant. The person in charge, Bernardino Zambotti, wrote the report in his own hand, because he was also a chronicler and a writer of the city's history:

> I, as the superior of the tax office, made two prostitutes of the public brothel receive two violent thrashings each from a rope, hanging from a pole set up in the Square, outside the windows of the *Podestà*, because they had harmed a peasant and taken from him a pair of shoes and a cap; and I made all the other prostitutes witness the spectacle.[6]

This was a spectacle precisely for the purpose of admonishing and dissuading behaviour of that kind, behaviour which, however, recurred in Ferrara and elsewhere. It is true, however, that the prostitutes sometimes lured clients by tearing the hats from their heads and immediately afterwards inviting them to come inside to take them back, and cheated or robbed them of their money. On a morning in June, from her studio-workshop in the large brothel complex of Verona, Pellegrina saw humanity passing by her window. First she got angry with a servant, a certain Domenico di Antonio, managing to snatch his "hat from his head" and with this trophy demand that "he screw her" in order to get it back, and then, perhaps unhappy about not getting what she wanted, she stole from a passing child a bunch of violets that he was holding in his hand. She did more than that. When he shouted at her, "Give me back my violets," she picked up a club and ran after him, calling him a "little thief" in a unique form of role reversal.[7]

The prostitutes' aggressiveness was focussed in the first place on their workmates. They insulted, pushed and shoved, kicked, and scratched each other, and sometimes caused more serious wounds, inflicted with cudgels or daggers. There were rivalries, intolerant behaviours, jealousies. In the Ferrara bordello, in June of 1458, Catherine, a Polish prostitute, hit a colleague with a big club; a few months later, in November, fiery words flew between Caterina from Siena and the German, Agnese, and then the two went on to use their hands, and in the end, the Italian threw a chair at the other, hitting her in the face and splitting her lip. A short time later, another furious fight broke out between the Slavonian, Maria, and the Venetian, Agnese.[8] In order for the women to get back to peaceful coexistence and prostituting themselves side by side, they entered into agreements and reconciliations, sworn in front of notaries, who were the guarantor-officials of a large part of the actions and transactions of medieval life. Having granted forgiveness for all offences and physical harassment, having pronounced a solemn commitment to not repeat these actions, and with all of these statements set down on paper before witnesses, and containing the notarial seal, the women returned to their everyday existence.

The women were violent with each other and arrogant with clients, but it is also true that some clients left without paying or tried to rob them and that many of the men assaulted them without apparent reason, hit them, struck them with whatever was at hand, disfigured them in a permanent way with knives and swords, made them bleed, marring them in such a way as to make them no longer desirable, no longer able to work. For this reason they predominantly aimed for the face, the throat, the chest, and hands, with cutting tools and sticks. They hit the women on the shoulders, legs, hips, causing contusions, lacerations, rendering the women's bodies swollen and painful for a long time. For some of them, these were signs that could never be erased, that sometimes left them handicapped, that would tell the story of their past. Marina, a Venetian prostitute, was used to the blows of her personal pimp. According to the account of the Decency officials in October 1452, he hit her regularly in the Florentine bordello where they had ended up staying, but in September of that year, in the bedroom in which she lived and worked, he crossed a line. With a piece of wood, he hit her many times on her shoulders, kidneys, arms, thigh, and foot. He made her bleed, and left her so swollen as to be unrecognizable. He had gone beyond the "normality" of the daily beating. His rage had inspired him to the point of revealing the way he worked, of demonstrating that his actions were no longer acceptable or defensible. The pimp was ordered to pay a 400 lire fine, of which only a quarter was destined for Marina as compensation. The rest would have filled the justice coffers, as long as the man would actually pay the fine.[9]

A public woman was an expert in men and their ways and in general was able to measure through experience someone's capacity for violence or inclination to steal, but she had to be very vigilant, ready to avoid falling into a trap, ready to expect the unexpected, and deal with the threat. Giovanna di Antonio, from Milan, had more than once transacted business with Domenico di Chele at the Pistoia bordello, and so he was not an unfamiliar client but a habitual frequenter whom she had probably come to trust. On the night of 12 August 1427, the man's violence took her completely by surprise. When he joined her in her room, she wasn't paying enough attention and was unaware of the razor and pincers that Domenico had hidden somewhere on his person. The pincers were to be used to break open a large strongbox that Giovanna kept in her room, and the razor was for her, perhaps for the purpose of intimidation or to kill her. His primary intention had been to steal. Once in bed, and grasping his weapon in his right hand, holding her head with his left, and with his arm blocking her shoulder, the man tried to bring his violent intentions to fruition, but Giovanna was faster. She saw the razor and managed to wriggle out of the bed while screaming at him. This reaction was so sudden and unforeseen that Domenico, more shocked than scared, dropped the razor. Giovanna picked it up, but before she could threaten him with it, Domenico began to confess and plead for forgiveness. Giovanna was charitable and gave him permission to leave without her calling for anyone, especially not the guards of the *podestà*. The man got dressed and put on his cloak, rather awkwardly, trying to hide the pincers from view, thus demonstrating another sign of his nefarious intentions. Again, however, he was caught in the act, questioned, and reprimanded. Crying, he threw himself onto his knees and again received her forgiveness and a farewell: "Be on your way, traitor," she generously commanded him. "Go with God and never appear wherever I may be."[10]

In Pisa, a year before, but in the same August summer heat, in the city's "little castle," the Parisian Maria was not able to intuit the evil intentions of a client nor escape his dagger, except perhaps to avoid a more serious injury. He cut her left shoulder instead of her throat, causing a wound *cum effusione sanguinis* (with an outpouring of blood), the distinctive expression to determine the seriousness of a lesion, fortunately a non-fatal one.[11] In the same place, which had been entrusted to the safekeeping of the brothel keeper and watched over by the public authority, something else happened, undoubtedly less serious, but significant in terms of the way in which public women were viewed and of the derisive contempt that was tolerated in relation to them. Any offence, humiliation, or insult suffered by a prostitute did not constitute a reason for censure, as it would have in the case of a woman of honour. And so, added to the scorn, we also have the awareness that all others, women and men, judged her to be deserving of these offences and undeserving of the right to any form of respect. But above all, there did not exist any safeguards and protections capable of stopping others from mistreating public women as they pleased. In the episode in question, Giovanni, a German, had urinated with absolute disregard near the door of the studio where a Venetian prostitute lived. She took objection, showed her annoyance, and reminded him that she paid a good deal of rent for her premises – thirteen cents a day – and therefore did not want anyone to defile it. "To spite you, I'll pee here, and I'll do even worse," replied the man. It was then that the exasperated Venetian woman took him by the arm and pushed him to the ground. In the ensuing fight, the man got the worst of it, receiving a blow above his eyebrow inflicted with a key that the prostitute held in her hand. Inasmuch as her jab to his head had not caused any blood flow, and therefore was considered less serious, and even though the woman had been provoked, insulted, and also hit during the altercation, the captain of Pisa convicted only her and absolved the instigator. She received a five lire fine, the equivalent of almost eight days rent for her room, for having rebelled with force against the abuse and for having sought to validate her course of action.[12] It is strange to read in these documents of accusation, in which the protagonists appear to be aggressive prostitutes or at least ones ready to defend themselves with a certain amount of belligerence, how the men always seem to surrender like victims, almost incapable of defending themselves against the female reaction, whereas initially they had been smug and violent.

It is possible that the prostitute learned to control her anger and submit to humiliation and prevaricate without protest once she paid the financial penalty. It would have been difficult, on the other hand, for her to resign herself to living with serious, mutilating, and disfiguring injuries that changed her quality of life, or rendered her handicapped, and prevented the only possibility of earning a living. Andriana di Marco from Venice was not able to defend herself nor had she expected to be assaulted since the assailant, Bernardino from Verona, had approached her studio with a friendly attitude, pretending to bend towards her in order to kiss her, but instead struck her with a sword, causing a horrible wound to her neck, at the height of her clavicle, cutting her cheek to the bone and also her right hand, in a gushing of blood that seemed to pour out of her like an unstoppable river. It was 25 October 1471 and the conviction from the Florentine magistracy of Decency was quick and hefty: a 250 florin fine and ten years of jail time if it wasn't paid within ten days. The woman was in fact left horribly disfigured and disabled, but a year and a half later the severity of the fine was reduced by a compromise. Andriana was forced to pardon her aggressor who went free after having paid, perhaps, part of the financial penalty.[13] With eight thrusts of a dagger, to the head, arms, hands and other parts of the body, Bartolomeo from Mantua wounded Caterina, called the Bresciana (being from Brescia), without any previous dispute or fight (which one can read in the document) while she was sitting on a chair at the door of her studio. And the Milanese weapons maker, also named Bartolomeo, caught another prostitute, Dorotea, a German, by surprise. She was quietly sitting inside her room when the man assaulted her with a sword – two well-delivered strikes, to the throat and face, caused permanent disfigurement.[14] The Florentine dyer Tommaso di Antonio attacked Margherita in the vicinity of her dwelling, first hitting her and then making use of a knife to wound her in the throat, face, and arms.[15]

Most often we do not know the reasons for these violently aggressive situations. Hard feelings, frustrations, complaints, and wrongs received can ignite anger and put weapons into the hands of those individuals, often clients or neighbours who revolved around prostitutes. The evidence does not reconstruct the course of events, only records the actions after they are already irreparable, and they do not weave the thread of a previous acquaintance, some bond, or temporary relationship in which the two people, victim and tormentor, brushed up against each other and perhaps were offended. On the other hand, the relationships between the prostitutes and pimps are clearly delineated. The latter felt they had a right to hit, punish, and whip for the least transgression, for having disobeyed their orders or behaving in a way the men believed they should not. They appealed to the agreements between them, to the bonds that united them, and claimed that their violence was justified and that it was proper to get rough on a regular basis. The Lombard Giovanni was the protector of the German Caterina, whom he beat wherever they were at the time – her room, the street, during the day, or night – causing contusions and making her bleed. For this he had been rebuked, without any significant result, by the Council of Decency. The Florentine Matteo preferred to beat his partner Giannetta, from France, when she was naked on the bed and to whip her until she bled. It is understandable that the woman decided at a certain point to pay him a large sum of money in order to separate from him and dissolve the heavy chain that bound her to a torturer.[16]

Certainly we cannot reduce the life of public women and their presence in brothels to a series of days characterized by violence and every kind of degradation. The episodes recounted here, and others that could be told, as far as the evidence can lead us, represent exceptions to the norm – namely, complaints made before tribunals, inquisitions, and condemnations. Moreover, since we do not have statistically significant data, we are not able to reconstruct how much these particular cases affected a different type of reality, in which perhaps we would be able to imagine a less traumatic existence for a public woman, a more satisfying one, more freely geared towards the exercise of a practice considered profitable and not humiliating. Certainly the figure of the sixteenth-century courtesan – elegant, cultured, sometimes loved, well compensated, and with an elevated standard of living – does not resemble that of the medieval prostitute, nor do the palaces where the courtesans sometimes lived have anything to do with the bordellos and studios overlooking the streets. The two figures cannot be confused nor must we forget that in medieval culture and imagination the public woman was a sinner and, as has been said, a corruptor. Her actions of enticing, soliciting, and tempting, in a way, absolved a man from the responsibility of his choices. These prostitutes even became the disposal ground of the contradictions of a society that scorned them, considered them unworthy, subjected them to disgraceful legislation, and exploited them but did not wish to do without them and, in order to justify its actions, constructed specious ideological frameworks, deceitful abstract principles, designed to legitimize an actual practice built on sexual needs and urges that required, in everyone's opinion, immediate and easy satisfaction.

12

Repentance

The road to repentance is paved with good intentions, resignation, and hope, and is also full of obstacles. Humility and perseverance are essential. And so is the conviction of having erred, of having dissipated one's existence, and that of others, in a life of sin. One has to believe in the possibility of redemption and obstinately seek a return to "living morally." After "a life of ill repute" comes "a life of good repute," here on earth, before the hope of eternal salvation. It is a solitary road that everyone must begin to travel out of conviction and choice and not out of an absence of alternatives or out of obligation. Old prostitutes – the term is relative and does not correspond at all to an objective aging – who through the passage of time had been stripped of charm, of the attractions of a young and desirable body, and deprived of opportunities and the means to work, without a home except for a room or studio in the brothel, without being able to count on any savings nor on an alternative occupation, were tossed aside like worn out objects. They saw their horizon of choices and concrete possibilities shrinking. Opening before them were the doors of the convents for the converted, houses of assistance, or charitable institutes founded in Europe's principal cities by generous philanthropists, clerics, monastic, and conventual orders, or by lay congregations. From the second half of the thirteenth century there was a flurry of initiatives and bequests to support these. While legalized systems for the exploitation of prostitutes were being built, spaces for contrition and repentance were concurrently being set up.

These were places designed for aged prostitutes without means of support or resources and primarily those wishing to abandon their profession and prior public life, ready to sever undesirable ties and by so doing put an end to a tormented existence. In the darkness surrounding them, preventing them from glimpsing any way out, even those chinks of flashing light from these open doorways was a tempting streak of luminosity. These were houses of assistance and of charitable hospitality, offered to people in difficulty but not without trade-offs. They were places of redemption and sacrifice into which one entered by renouncing one's past and recognizing one's guilt. These were all female journeys: the moral downfall, the life of excess and perdition, followed by remorse, correction, and penitence lived in solitude. Taking responsibility and accepting blame did not compromise the male conscience.

In 1272, in Marseille, a certain Bertrand founded a religious congregation of Augustinians with a mission to convert prostitutes to a life of penitence and faith. Welcomed into pious houses, they became penitents. Penitents, converted, *filles repenties* (penitent girls) – with these designations allusion was made to public women admitted to institutions that took their names from them or were named after Saint Mary Magdalene, Saint Elisabeth, or Saint Mary of Egypt. In Paris, it was the Hôpital de la Madeleine in 1316 and in 1492, the conservatory of the Filles Pénitentes; in Grenoble, the Hôpital of the Filles Repenties in 1458; in Naples, in 1324, the convent of Saint Mary Magdalene and then of Santa Mary of Egypt; in Florence, at the beginning of the fifteenth century, the convent of Saint Elisabeth or of the Converted. In Vienna, in 1384, they were shelters for "poor women who wish to abandon public life and better themselves" opened in mutual agreement by three citizens.[1]

These were men who had contributed to the condemnation of the prostitutes and then wanted to save them. But salvation is not for everyone, and it is not a gift but rather a summit to be reached through effort, deprivation, penance, atonement, and, when necessary, punishment. One did not enter and, more importantly, one did not stay in these houses without complying to precise rules, paying tax, depositing an endowment, bringing witnesses of one's conversion, and committing oneself to a program of rehabilitation that anticipated the renunciation of sins and the past in exchange for a life of austerity and strictness, chastity and isolation. Every step in the process had been defined and would be closely monitored. Every decision was subjected to close inspection by confession and communion. The testimony produced in one's favour had to be supported by other proofs, chosen by public officials. The sincerity of the transformation had to be put to the test through months of examination. Only after having passed through all the obstacles with which the path was strewn, could one be deleted from the list of public prostitutes.

These shelters and houses of assistance were based on a secular initiative, although of mixed management and with the presence of religious individuals, and shared basic principles of reeducation but also offered the prospect of reintegration into society as an alternative to permanent confinement. Public women who had repudiated their past were taught a trade and upon completion of this training were given opportunities to find employment outside the shelter. For some it was even possible to anticipate marriage arranged by the institution and with the payment of a dowry, acquired through working within the home or from a donation. Men of the lower class, with meagre incomes, would have found these allocations of money a convincing reason to marry an exprostitute. These types of institutions were more successful and widespread from the sixteenth century on, while during the centuries of the late Middle Ages more reliance was placed on religious establishments.

The convents of the penitent were, generally speaking, controlled from the outside by collegiate bodies in which representatives from religious and lay powers, appointed by the government, took part. Internally, the convents were managed by a female hierarchy with the top position held by an abbess. The place, in fact, accommodated women in diverse positions.

There were laywomen, simple converts, sisters in service to their companions, those who had taken their vows and who participated in the management of the convent, and, finally, above all of these, the "mother superiors."[2] The constant that united them was that of being the poorest of the religious institutions, the ones that received the smallest endowments and struggled to survive with the help of the residents' manual labour and private donations. Within the internal hierarchy, penitent prostitutes generally occupied the lowest positions, sometimes at the service of their sisters, daily fighting a hard battle to demonstrate the sincerity of their repentance, and accepting hardships, mortifications, and humiliations while resisting every form of false hope and temptation from their previous life of prostitution where their past exploiters were not resigned to lost revenues, and continually tried to get them to return to the business so that they might recuperate their sources of income. What had once seemed at times intolerable, in the indistinctness of memory, was luring them back, and the appeal was hard to resist. Even with the desire to recant, forget, and distance themselves from the past, attempts at abduction from the outside were continuous, as were other insistent requests of every kind. The pimps, and more rarely the brothel keepers, reminded them of their relationships of old, belatedly pretended feelings they had never shown previously and boasted of nonexistent assets. They used their ingenuity in every possible way to get the woman, who they considered their property, to leave the refuge of the convent. Once these men were sent away by the nuns and the interested parties themselves, and were cautioned by public officials, they persevered in their harassment by resorting to intermediaries above suspicion, those who had free access to the building: women, artisans, workers responsible for some service, who volunteered to secretly bring in a written note or report some message. This psychological violence, this wearing assault from the outside, hindered the detachment and tranquillity that the penitent prostitutes sought and which they thought they had acquired. In order to earn some peace and not fall back into the old life, a woman might sometimes pay an expimp money she did not owe him as a kind of liquidation or compensatory amount for having deprived him of his remunerative capital – herself and her body.

Demands and illegitimate requests might also come from operators of disreputable taverns, and unprincipled women, who went in search of prostitutes to offer up to a private clientele outside the bordello circuit. The converted prostitutes, both young and less young, seemed the perfect prey since they were fragile, easy victims of blackmail and intimidation, and sometimes indecisive. They had ended up in the shelters or convents in order to escape violence or a debt too high to pay. They may not have had the conviction and tenacious will needed to acknowledge before everyone – their companions as well as themselves – to have lived in scandal and sin, to have led a shameful existence, to have lost honour and dignity, of which they were constantly reminded and reproached. If the intention was to come to the aid of public women, to help them escape the world of prostitution and reinvent themselves, the contemplated path did not envisage indulgence, understanding, or solidarity of any kind, and the method was merciless. Would there ever be an end to the admissions of guilt, the demoralization inherent in repentance, self-punishment, and chastisement or were these things to last forever? And if at one time these women were received, recognized, registered, and organized as necessary and indispensable to the social order, to the safety of their moral and virtuous sisters, and to the defence of male violence – this, too, a well-disguised deception – why did they have to continue to pay the price for a choice that sometimes they hadn't even shared in and which had led them to live a wretched existence mostly benefiting men: the clients, pimps, and brothel keepers?

Once again the individual destinies, personal experiences, feelings, and consciousness of each woman were forced to defer to the current mentality, social norm, and power of institutions. Just like the act of prostituting oneself, repenting seems to be a page written by others, a script predetermined and not the result of a journey of reflection or a voluntary choice. If in medieval culture prostitution was a necessary evil and the prostitute an indispensible instrument, the obligation to repent having lived a "life of ill repute" was, nevertheless, imposed upon the women, as well as the obligation to convert to a good life through renunciation, remorse, and contrition, in most cases, at the end of their career, when they had completed their task. In the final analysis, the ambiguities and contradictions of the beginnings were never resolved through the many centuries of good governance by states and policies of the church.

Notes

CHAPTER ONE

1 For some of these expressions, see E. Lacarra Lanz, "Legal and Clandestine Prostitution in Medieval Spain," *Bulletin of Hispanic Studies* 79 (2002): 265–85; D.Y. Ghirardo, "Topography of Prostitution in Renaissance Ferrara," *Journal of the Society of Architectural Historians* 60, 4 (2001): 401–31; A. Gamba, "La prostituzione a Ferrara nel tardo medioevo" (doctoral dissertation, Università degli Studi di Ferrara, 1996–97).

2 A. Fabretti, *La prostituzione in Perugia nei secoli XIV, XV e XVI* (Turin: s.e., 1890), 9.

3 L.L. Otis, *Prostitution in Medieval Society: The History of an Urban Institution in Languedoc* (Chicago: The University of Chicago Press, 1985), 49–50.

4 Lacarra Lanz, "Legal and Clandestine Prostitution."

5 Ibid. See as well, by the same author, "Evolución de la prostitución en la Castilla del siglo XV y la mancebía de Salamanca en tiempos de Fernando de Rojas," in *Approaching the Fifth Centenary*, edited by I.A. Corfis and J.T. Snow (Madison, WI: Hispanic Seminary of Medieval Studies, 1993), 33–78.

6 J. Rossiaud, *Amori venali. La prostituzione nell'Europa medievale* (Rome-Bari: Laterza, 2013), 86–7.

7 See S. Raveggi, "Il lessico delle ingiurie contro le donne," in *Violenza alle donne*, edited by A. Esposito, F. Franceschi, and G. Piccinni (Bologna: Il Mulino, 2018), 129–49.

8 Archivio di Stato di Firenze (State Archives of Florence, hereafter ASF), *Miscellanea Repubblicana*, 33, c. 53.

9 Raveggi, "Il lessico delle ingiurie," 145.
10 Niccolò Machiavelli, *Lettere*, edited by F. Gaeta (Milano: Feltrinelli, 1981), n108, 204–6.
11 See S. Tramontana, "La meretrice," in *Condizione umana e ruoli sociali nel Mezzogiorno normanno-svevo*, proceedings of the IX Giornate normanno-sveve (Bari: Dedalo, 1989 and 1991), 79–101.
12 It is Rossiaud who tells us this story in *Amori venali*, 120–1. Pero Tafur, *Travels and Adventures*, 1435–39, edited by M. Letts (London: Routledge, 1926).

CHAPTER TWO

1 M.G. Muzzarelli, *Una componente della mentalità occidentale: i penitenziali nell'alto MedioEvo* (Bologna: Patron, 1980).
2 R.L. Ménager, "Sesso e repressione: quando, perché. Una risposta della storia giuridica," *Quaderni medievali*, 4 (1977): 47–52.
3 G. Duby, *Il cavaliere, la donna, il prete* (Rome-Bari: Laterza, 1982), 51–65.
4 M.G. Muzzarelli, *Pescatori di uomini. Predicatori e piazze alla fine del Medioevo* (Bologna: Il Mulino), 2005.
5 J.A. Brundage, *Law, Sex and Christian Society in Medieval Europe* (Chicago: The University of Chicago Press, 1987); G. Duby, *I peccati delle donne nel Medioevo* (Rome-Bari: Laterza, 1999).
6 Duby, *I peccati delle donne nel Medioevo* (Rome-Bari: Laterza, 1999), 29.
7 Ibid. and Duby, *Il cavaliere, la donna, il prete*, 19–24.
8 Sancti Antonini Archiepiscopi, *Summa Theologica in quattuor partes distribuita* (Veronae, MDCCXL, riprod. Graz., 1959), *pars secunda, titulus V, de luxuria*.
9 Umberto da Romans, *Prediche alle donne del secolo XIII*, edited by C. Casagrande (Milan: Bompiani, 1978), 29–32.
10 Cherubino da Siena, *Regola della vita matrimoniale*, edited by F. Zambrini and C. Negroni (Bologna, 1888, facsimile reprint 1968), 107–12.
11 Rossiaud, *Amori venali*, 13 and 140.
12 M. Pilosu, "L'atteggiamento della Chiesa medievale verso la prostituzione. Continuità e novità nei secoli XII e XIII," *Studi storico-religiosi* 6, 1–2 (1982): 143–62 and in particular 143–4. By the same author, see also *La donna, la lussuria e la Chiesa nel Medioevo* (Genoa: ECIG, 1989). J.A. Brundage, "Prostitution in the Medieval Canon Law," *Signs* 1, 4 (1976): 825–45.

13 Giordano da Pisa, *Quaresimale fiorentino (1305–1306)*, edited by C. Delcorno (Florence: Sansoni, 1974), 210.
14 See Duby, *Il cavaliere, la donna, il prete*, 146.
15 Tramontana, *La meretrice*.
16 Bernardino da Siena, *Prediche volgari sul Campo di Siena, 1427*, edited by C. Delcorno (Milano: Rusconi, 1989), 2 volumes, XXXIX, volume II, 894; XIX, volume I, 140; XXXV, volume II, 796–7.
17 Pilosu, "L'atteggiamento della Chiesa medievale verso la prostituzione," 150–1, 152–4, 161–2.

CHAPTER THREE

1 On this subject, see E. Crouzet-Pavan, "Police des moeurs, société et politique à Venise à la fin du Moyen Âge," *Revue historique* 264 (1980): 241–88; E. Crouzet-Pavan, "Violence, société et pouvoir à Venise (XIV–XV siècles): forme et évolution de rituels urbains," *Mélanges de l'École Française de Rome, Moyen Âge* 2 (1984): 903–36; E. Crouzet-Pavan, *Sopra le acque salse. Espaces, pouvoir et société à Venise à la fin du Moyen Âge* (Rome: École Française de Rome, 1992); E. Crouzet-Pavan, "Un fior del male: i giovani nelle società urbane italiane, secoli XIV–XV," in *Storia dei giovani*, edited by J.C. Schmitt and G. Levi (Rome-Bari: Laterza, 1994), t.I, 211–77; G. Ruggiero, *I confini dell'eros.Crimini sessuali e sessualità nella Venezia del Rinascimento* (Venice: Marsilio, 1987); G. Ruggiero, *Patrizi e malfattori. La violenza a Venezia nel primo Rinascimento* (Bologna: Il Mulino, 1982).
2 For an example, see ASF, *Provvisioni, Registri*, 119, cc. 69r70v, 18 June 1428: the protagonists were between twelve and thirteen years of age.
3 ASF, *Giudice degli Appelli, Ufficiali intrinseci*, 75, cc. 147r and v, 10 February 1426.
4 T.M. Vinyoles Vidal, *La violència marginal a les ciutats medievals (exemples a la Barcelona dels volts del 1400)*, in the "Revista d'història medieval," *Violència i marginaciò en la societat medieval* 1 (1990), 177.
5 M.J. Rocke, *Il controllo dell'omosessualità a Firenze nel XV secolo: gli Ufficiali di Notte*, in the "Quaderni storici," LXVI, 3, 1987, 701–23, in particular 101; M.J. Rocke, *Forbidden Friendships: Homosexuality and Male Culture in Renaissance Florence* (New York and Oxford: Oxford University Press, 1996); Ruggiero, *I confini dell'eros*; Ruggiero, *Patrizi e malfattori*; R. Canosa, *Storia di una grande paura. La sodomia a Firenze e a Venezia nel Quattrocento* (Milan: Feltrinelli, 1991).

6 Vidal, *La violència marginal a les ciutats medievals*, 177.
7 Rocke, *Il controllo dell'omosessualità a Firenze nel XV secolo*, in particular 101; Rocke, *Forbidden Friendships*; Ruggiero, *I confini dell'eros*; Ruggiero, *Patrizi e malfattori*; Canosa, *Storia di una grande paura.*
8 ASF, *Provvisioni, Registri*, 108, c. 2v.
9 A. Garosi, *Siena nella storia della medicina, 1240–1555* (Florence: Olschki, 1958).
10 ASF, *Provvisioni, Registri*, 120, cc. 62v–3v.
11 ASF, *Provvisioni, Registri*, 138, December 1447.
12 See Duby, *I peccati delle donne*, 87; the sermons were collected and published in 1226.
13 Rossiaud, *Amori venali*, 15–20.

CHAPTER FOUR

1 L.L. Otis, *Prostitution in Medieval Society: The History of an Urban Institution in Languedoc* (Chicago: The University of Chicago Press, 1985), 265–7.
2 See J. Rossiaud, *Amori venali. La prostituzione nell'Europa medievale* (Rome-Bari: Laterza, 2013), 73–5.
3 ASF, *Acquisti e doni*, 294.
4 For this episode see ASF, *Provvisioni, Registri*, 116, cc. 10v–11r, 27 March 1426: one example among many. On the reality and function of the taverns, see G. Cherubini, "La taverna nel basso Medioevo," in *Il tempo libero. Economia e società, secc. XIII - XVIII, XXVI* settimana di Studi, Prato, 18–23 April 1994, edited by Cavaciocchi (Florence: Le Monnier, 1995), 525–55.
5 Rossiaud, *Amori venali*, 79–81.
6 A. Lisini, ed., *Il Constituto del Comune di Siena volgarizzato nel 1309–1310* (Siena: Tip. Lazzeri, 1903, II, V, r. XLV), 252. See the most recent critical edition, edited by M.S. Elsheikh (Siena: Fondazione del Monte dei Paschi, 2002).
7 ASF, *Otto di Guardia*, n55, c. 58v, 9 May 1480 and n68, c. 134v, 31 October 1484: the second time they received a heavy fine if they took down the wall and the recently closed door was reopened.
8 E. Diana, *Sanità nel quotidiano* (Florence: Lucio Pugliese, 1995), 131–2.
9 Rossiaud, *Amori venali*, 78.
10 ASF, *Giudice degli appelli, Ufficiali intrinseci*, n83, c144, 31 August 1452; ibid., n77, c240, 28 October 1430.

11 Paolo da Certaldo, *Libro di buoni costumi*, edited by A. Schiaffini (Florence: Le Monnier, 1945), 63.
12 ASF, *Capitano del Popolo*, 35, cXXVI, a1346.
13 E. Crouzet-Pavan, "Police des moeurs, société et politique à Venise à la fin du Moyen Âge," *Revue historique* 264 (1980): 258–61.
14 ASF, *Acquisti e doni*, 294, February 1496/7.
15 ASF, *Provvisioni, Registri*, 159, cc. 67r and v.
16 C. Delcorno, "L' 'exemplum' nella predicazione di Bernardino da Siena," in *Bernardino predicatore nella società del suo tempo, Proceedings of the Fifteenth Conference of the Centre for the Study of Medieval Spirituality*, 9–12 October 1975 (Todi: Accademia Tudertina, 1976), 71–107, here 86 and n1.
17 Bernardino da Siena, *Prediche volgari sul Campo di Siena, 1427*, edited by C. Delcorno (Milano: Rusconi, 1989), 2 volumes, XXII, volume I, 637–8.
18 ASF, *Otto di Guardia*, 68, cc. 25v–26, 21 July 1484: Antonia of Brescia sold a *puellam* (girl) of thirteen years after having forced her to prostitute herself in a Florentine brothel.
19 A. Esposito, "Violenza psicologica, violenza fisica. Donne a Roma e nello Stato Pontificio," in *Violenza alle donne*, edited by A. Esposito, F. Franceschi, and G. Piccinni (Bologna: Il Mulino, 2018), 209–31, in particular, 215–16.
20 M. Gazzini, "La violenza e la grazia. Storie di donne e di crimini nel ducato di Milano," Esposito, Franceschi, and Piccinni, *Violenza alle donne*, 233–54, in particular, 241–6.
21 M.S. Mazzi, *Donne in fuga* (Bologna: Il Mulino, 2017), 170.
22 See F. Franceschi and L. Molà, *Discriminazione, sopraffazione, violenza nel mondo del lavoro*, in Esposito, Franceschi, and Piccinni, *Violenza alle donne*, 57–84. On women's work, see M.P. Zanoboni, *Donne al lavoro nell'Italia e nell'Europa medievali (secoli XIII-XV)* (Milano: Jouvence, 2016).

CHAPTER FIVE

1 M. Pilosu, "L'atteggiamento della Chiesa medievale verso la prostituzione. Continuità e novità nei secoli XII e XIII," *Studi storico-religiosi* 6, 1–2 (1982): 143.
2 ASF, *Giudice degli Appelli*, n67, n.c.
3 G.A. Brucker, *Firenze nel Rinascimento* (Florence: La Nuova Italia, 1980), 351–4. The year was 1400.

4 E. Lacarra Lanz, "Legal and clandestine prostitution in medieval Spain," *Bulletin of Hispanic Studies* 79 (2002): 17–19.

CHAPTER SIX

1 M.G. Muzzarelli, *Guardaroba medievale* (Bologna: Il Mulino, 1999), 288.
2 Ibid., 247–333, in particular, 273 and by the same author, *Gli inganni delle apparenze* (Turin: Paravia, 1996), with references to the sumptuary laws on 99–154.
3 Otis, *Prostitution in Medieval Society*.
4 See A. Gamba, "La prostituzione a Ferrara nel tardo medioevo" (dissertation, Università degli Studi di Ferrara, 1996–97), 37–40; R. Canosa and I. Colonnello, *Storia della prostituzione in Italia: dal Quattrocento alla fine del Settecento* (Rome: Sapere 2000, 1989), 23; S. Arcuti, *Segnate a vista: donne di strada nel Medioevo* (Lecce, Brescia: Pensa Multimedia, 2001).
5 Lisini, *Il Constituto del Comune di Siena volgarizzato nel 1309–1310*, II, III, r. CCLIII, 111–12; ibid., V, 250–1; ibid., V, r. XXV, 244.
6 G. Camerani Marri, ed., *Statuto di Arezzo (1327)* (Firenze: Olschki, 1946, 2008 reprint), l. IV, r. LXIIII, 227.
7 M.S. Mazzi, "Un 'dilettoso luogo': l'organizzazione della prostituzione nel tardo medioevo," in *Città e servizi sociali nell'Italia dei secoli XII-XV, XII*, convegno di Studi, Pistoia, 9–12 October 1987 (Pistoia: office of the centre, 1990), 469.
8 A. Grohmann, *Città e territorio fra Medioevo ed età moderna* (Perugia: Volumnia, 1982), 319–21.
9 Arcuti, *Segnate a vista*; Canosa and Colonnello, *Storia della prostituzione in Italia*; G. Rezasco, *Segno delle meretrici* (Genoa: Tipografia dell'Istituto Sordomuti, 1890); J.A. Brundage, "Sumptuary Laws and Prostitution in late Medieval Italy," *Journal of Medieval History* 13 (1987): 343–55; Muzzarelli, *Guardaroba medievale*, 287–97.
10 Ibid., 287.
11 ASF, *Onestà*, 1, cc. 21r and v, 8 April 1511.
12 Lacarra Lanz, "Legal and clandestine prostitution."
13 Rossiaud, *Amori venali*, 253–61.
14 Tramontana, "La meretrice," in *Condizione umana e ruoli sociali nel Mezzogiorno normanno-svevo*, proceedings from the IX Giornate normanno-sveve (Bari: Dedalo, 1989 and 1991), 93.

15 Rossiaud, *Amori venali*, 157 and A. Fabretti, *La prostituzione in Perugia nei secoli XIV, XV and XVI* (Turin: s.e., 1890), 93.

CHAPTER SEVEN

1 E. Artifoni, *I ribaldi. Immagini e istituzioni della marginalità nel tardo medioevo* (Torino: Einaudi, 1985); J. Rossiaud, *La prostituzione nel Medioevo* (Roma-Bari: Laterza, 1984), 76–7 and Rossiaud, *Amori venali*, 253; R. Comba, "'Apetitus libidinis coherceatur': strutture demografiche, reati sessuali e disciplina dei comportamenti nel Piemonte tardomedievale," *Studi Storici* 27 (1986): 566–7; G. Ortalli, ed., *Gioco e giustizia nell'Italia di Comune* (Treviso-Rome: Viella, 1993), 100; R. Rinaldi, "'Mulieres publicae': Testimonianze e note sulla prostituzione tra pieno e tardo Medioevo," in *Donne e lavoro nell'Italia medievale*, edited by M.G. Muzzarelli, P. Galetti, and B. Andreolli (Turin: Rosenberg & Sellier, 1991), 105–25.

2 Lacarra Lanz, "Legal and clandestine prostitution."

3 Lisini, *Il Constituto del Comune di Siena volgarizzato nel 1309–1310*, II, V, r. DXI, 475.

4 Rinaldi, "'Mulieres publicae.'"

5 Gamba, "La prostituzione a Ferrara," 117–19, 127, and 128.

6 Ibid., 137 and 138.

7 M.S. Mazzi, *Prostitute e lenoni nella Firenze del Quattrocento* (Milano: Il Saggiatore, 1991), 202–3.

8 ASF, *Giudice degli Appelli, Ufficiali intrinseci*, 74, cc. 235v236r, 13 May 1415, he was found guilty and fined 100 lire, namely twenty-five florins.

CHAPTER EIGHT

1 In Tarrascon, the brothel, built in 1374, was enlarged in 1390 and enhanced in 1449; in Sisteron, it was planned in 1394 and built in 1424; in Villefranche-sur-Saône it was opened in 1438 and enlarged in 1454; in Bourg-en-Bresse it was functional from 1439 on; while in Tours and Amiens it opened in 1449. In Toulouse, the authorities took responsibility for the venture only in 1372, in Castres in 1391, in Albi in 1393. See J. Rossiaud, *Amori venali. La prostituzione nell'Europa medievale* (Rome-Bari: Laterza, 2013), 15–16; L.L. Otis, *Prostitution in Medieval Society: The History of an Urban Institution in Languedoc* (Chicago: University of Chicago Press, 1985); V. Bullough

and B. Bullough, *Women and Prostitution: A Social History* (Buffalo, NY: Prometheus, 1987).

2 See M.C. Peris, "La prostitución valenciana en la segunda mitad del siglo XIV," *Revista d'història medieval*, 1 (1990): 179–99 and E. Lacarra Lanz, "Legal and clandestine prostitution in medieval Spain," *Bulletin of Hispanic Studies* 79 (2002): 265–85; Lacarra Lanz, "Evolución de la prostitucion en la Castilla del siglo XV y la mancebìa de Salamanca en tiempos de Fernando de Rojas," in *Fernando de Rojas and Celestina: Approaching the Fifth Centenary*, edited by I.A. Corfis and J.T. Snow (Madison, WI: Hispanic Seminary of Medieval Studies); M. Asenjo González, "Las mujeres en el medio urbano a fines de la Edad Media: el caso de Segovia," in *Las mujeres en las ciudades medievales* (Universidad Autónoma de Madrid, Seminario de Estudios de la Mujer, 1984); V. Graullera, "Los hostaleros del burdel de Valencia," *Revista d'història medieval* 1 (1990): 201–13; F. Vázquez García and A. Moreno Mengíbar, *Poder y prostitucion en Sevilla* (Sevilla: Universidad de Sevilla, 1998), 2 volumes, with a useful bibliography on prostitution in Spain entitled "Bibliografía sobre la historia de la prostitución en España. La prostitución en la España medieval y moderna."

3 R. Canosa and I. Colonnello, *Storia della prostituzione in Italia: dal Quattrocento alla fine del Settecento* (Rome: Sapere 2000, 1989), 15.

4 Ibid., 23. R. Comba, "'Apetitus libidinis coherceatur': strutture demografiche, reati sessuali e disciplina dei comportamenti nel Piemonte tardo medievale," *Studi Storici* 27 (1986): 529–76; R. Rinaldi, "'Mulieres publicae.' Testimonianze e note sulla prostituzione tra pieno e tardo Medioevo," in *Donne e lavoro nell'Italia medievale*, edited by M.G. Muzzarelli, P. Galetti, and B. Andreolli (Turin: Rosenberg & Sellier, 1991).

5 E. Crouzet-Pavan, "Police des moeurs, société et politique à Venise à la fin du Moyen Âge," *Revue historique* 264 (1980): 241–88; G. Scarabello, *Meretrices. Storia della prostituzione a Venezia tra XII e XVIII secolo* (Venezia Lido: Supernova, 2008).

6 D. Balestracci and G. Piccinni, *Siena nel Trecento* (Florence: CLUSF, 1977), 60–1; Alcide Garosi, *Siena nella storia della medicina, 1240–1555* (Florence: Olschki, 1958), 520–2. In Pistoia, on the other hand, during the session of the Council of the Elders held in 1345, a provision for the choice of a suitable place for accommodating prostitutes was established: see A. Zanelli, "Le 'donne cortesi' a Pistoia," *Bullettino storico pistoiese* 3, 4 (1901): 142–4. While in Florence, legis-

lation was initiated on the regulation of prostitution since 1403, and in the first two decades of the fifteenth century, the brothel neighbourhood became operational: see. R. Trexler, *La prostitution florentine au XV siècle: patronages et clìenteles*, in the "Annales ESC," 36 (1981): 983–1015; M.S. Mazzi, "Un 'dilettoso luogo': l'organizzazione della prostituzione nel tardo medioevo," in *Città e servizi sociali nell'Italia dei secoli XII-XV*, Twelfth conference of Studies, Pistoia, 9–12 October 1987, at the headquarters of the centre, 1990, 465–80. In 1359, in Perugia, the bordello was already set up and was licensed under concession by the municipality with substantial profit. See A. Fabretti, *La prostituzione in Perugia nei secoli XIV, XV e XVI* (Turin: s.e., 1890); A. Grohmann, *Città e territorio fra Medioevo ed età moderna* (Perugia: Volumnia, 1982 (rist. anast. 2006), 319–21.

7 A. Cutrera, *Storia della prostituzione in Sicilia* (Palermo: ESA, 1971).

8 Rossiaud, *Amori venali*, 141.

9 D. Stiefelmeier, "Sacro e profano: note sulla prostituzione nella Germania medievale," *Nuova DWF*, 3 (1977): 34–50.

10 Peris, "La prostitutión valenciana"; Graullera, "Los hostaleros del burdel de Valencia"; and M.S. Mazzi, "Aspetti della prostituzione (secoli XIV–XV)," in *Il tempo libero. Economia e società* XXVI week of Studies, Prato, 18–23 April 1994, edited by S. Cavaciocchi (Florence: Le Monnier, 1995), 721–30, here 721.

11 Rossiaud, *Amori venali*, 141–2.

12 Canosa and Colonnello, *Storia della prostituzione in Italia*; ASF, *Provvisioni, Registri*, 119, cc. 205v–6v, 30 September 1428.

13 M.S. Mazzi, *Prostitute e lenoni nella Firenze del Quattrocento* (Milan: Il Saggiatore, 1991), 251–4.

14 Crouzet-Pavan, "Police des moeurs," 243–55.

15 A. Gamba, "La prostituzione a Ferrara nel tardo medioevo" (doctoral thesis, Università degli Studi di Ferrara, 1996–97), 336–7, 339–40.

16 Graullera, "Los hostaleros del burdel de Valencia," 201–3.

17 Rossiaud, *Amori venali*, 144–8.

18 Ibid., 150.

19 ASF, *Catasto*, 1427, 52, cc. 317r–323v and 289, II, 1451, cc. 552r and 554v.

20 ASF, *Catasto*, 1480, n1019, II, c. 6r.

21 ASF, *Catasto*, 1427, 52, cc. 263r–266v.

22 ASF, *Catasto*, 1019, c. 345.

23 Zanelli, "Le 'donne cortesi' a Pistoia," 144–5.

24 Mazzi, *Prostitute e lenoni nella Firenze del Quattrocento*, 259–60: this

concerns the furnishings of ten studios and four small rooms. The quantity of rooms in relation to the scarcity of objects leads one to think that some were truly bare.

25 Crouzet-Pavan, "Police des moeurs," 246–9.

26 Zanelli, "Le 'donne cortesi' a Pistoia," 145–6.

27 ASF, *Provvisioni, Registri*, 119, cc. 205v–6v.

28 ASF, *Catasto*, 52, cc. 317r–323v.

29 ASF, *Catasto*, 289, II, cc. 552r and 554v.

CHAPTER NINE

1 ASF, *Acquisti e doni,* 294, 7 July 1488.

2 ASF, *Otto di Guardia*, 68, cc. 49v–50r, 13 August 1484.

3 M.S. Mazzi, "La violenza sulle donne pubbliche," in *Violenza alle donne*, edited by A. Esposito, F. Franceschi,and G. Piccinni (Bologna: Il Mulino, 2018), 95.

4 Graullera, "Los hostaleros del burdel de Valencia," 204, 205.

5 S. Arcuti, *Segnate a vista: donne di strada nel Medioevo* (Lecce-Brescia: Pensa Multimedia, 2011); Canosa and Colonnello, *Storia della prostituzione in Italia*.

6 Mazzi, *Prostitute e lenoni nella Firenze del Quattrocento*.

7 Fabretti, *La prostituzione in Perugia*, 27–41.

8 Lacarra Lanz, "Legal and Clandestine Prostitution."

9 Ibid., 16.

10 Gamba, "La prostituzione a Ferrara," 158.

11 Ibid., 241.

12 Mazzi, *Prostitute e lenoni nella Firenze del Quattrocento*, 327–8.

CHAPTER TEN

1 V. Graullera, "Los hostaleros del burdel de Valencia," *Revista d'història medieval* 1 (1990): 190–1.

2 A. Gamba, "La prostituzione a Ferrara nel tardo medioevo" (dissertation, 1996–97, Università degli Studi di Ferrara), 239.

3 A. Cutrera, *Storia della prostituzione in Sicilia* (Palermo: ESA, 1971), 69.

4 For the Italian area see F. Franceschi and I. Taddei, *Le città italiane nel Medioevo, XII-XIV secolo* (Bologna: Il Mulino, 2012) and F. Franceschi, *"E saremo tutti ricchi." Lavoro, mobilità sociale, conflitti nelle città dell'Italia medievale* (Pisa: Pacini, 2012).

5 M.S. Mazzi, *Prostitute e lenoni nella Firenze del Quattrocento* (Milan: Il Saggiatore, 1991), 293–9.
6 J. Rossiaud, *Amori venali. La prostituzione nell'Europa medievale* (Rome-Bari: Laterza, 2013), 179–80.
7 R. Canosa and I. Colonnello, *Storia della prostituzione in Italia: dal Quattrocento alla fine del Settecento* (Rome: Sapere 2000, 1989), 16.
8 Rossiaud, *Amori venali*, 181 and 317.
9 A. Fabretti, *La prostituzione in Perugia nei secoli XIV, XV e XVI* (Turin: s.e., 1890), 87–8.
10 Ibid., 88 and 89.
11 Rossiaud, *Amori venali*, 177–8 and 303.
12 M.C. Peris, "La prostitución valenciana en la segunda mitad del siglo XV," *Revista d'història medieval*, 1 (1990): 179–99. E. Lacarra Lanz, "Evolución de la prostitución en la Castilla del siglo XV y la mancebìa de Salamanca en tiempos de Fernando de Rojas," in *Fernando de Rojas and Celestina: Approaching the Fifth Centenary*, edited by I.A. Corfis and J.T. Snow (Madison: WI, Hispanic Seminary of Medieval Studies, 1993), 33–78; E. Lacarra Lanz, "Legal and clandestine prostitution in medieval Spain," *Bulletin of Hispanic Studies* 79 (200), and Graullera, "Los hostaleros del burdel de Valencia."
13 ASF, Notarile Antecosimiano, T. 526, c. 94
14 Mazzi, *Prostitute e lenoni nella Firenze del Quattrocento*, 345–6.
15 Ibid., 342.
16 Ibid., 344.
17 Gamba, "La prostituzione a Ferrara," 262.
18 Ibid., 263–4.
19 Ibid.
20 Rossiaud, *Amori venali*, 53–5.

CHAPTER ELEVEN

1 Girolamo Savonarola, *Prediche sopra Amos e Zaccaria*, edited by P. Ghiglieri (Rome: Belardetti, 1971), I, sermon XII, 311–38, here, 322–4.
2 C. Cipolla and G. Malacarne, eds, *Amore e sesso al tempo dei Gonzaga* (Milan: Franco Angeli, 2006).
3 Fabretti, *La prostituzione in Perugia*, 93; M.G. Muzzarelli, *Guardaroba medievale* (Bologna: Il Mulino, 1999), 287.
4 Peris, "La prostitución valenciana," 192–3.

5 See Gamba, "La prostituzione a Ferrara," 272.
6 Bernardino Zambotti, "Diario ferrarese dall'anno 1476 sino al 1504," in *Rerum Italicarum Scriptores, XXIV*, edited by G. Pardi, second edition, section VII (Bologna: Nicola Zanichelli, 1934–37), 209.
7 ASF, *Onestà*, 2, cc. 104r and v. The woman was sentenced to pay five florins.
8 Gamba, "La prostituzione a Ferrara," 272.
9 ASF, *Giudice degli Appelli, Ufficiali intrinseci*, 83, cc. 167r and v, 10 October 1452.
10 Ibid., 76, cc. 401r–2r
11 Ibid., cc. 111v–112r.
12 Ibid., c. 34v.
13 ASF, *Onestà*, 2, cc. 80r–80v and *Provvisioni, Registri*, 164.
14 ASF, *Giudice degli Appelli, Ufficiali intrinseci*, 81, cc. 50r and v, 6 April 1446 and ibid., 82, cc. 299r–300v, 30 January 1447/8.
15 Ibid., 83, cc. 282r–283v, 7 May 1453.
16 Ibid., 84, cc. 28r and v, 28 August 1456, and *Miscellanea Repubblicana*, 33, cc. 11v and 52v, 16 August 1436.

REPENTANCE

1 M.S. Mazzi, *Donne in fuga* (Bologna: Il Mulino, 2017), 117.
2 See. S. Cohen, "Convertite e malmaritate. Donne 'irregolari' e ordini religiosi nella Firenze rinascimentale," *Memoria*, 5 (1982):46–63; G. Castelnovo, "'Malefemmine' Onore perduto, peccato espiato, corpi ammansiti" (doctoral thesis, University of Grenoble and University of Milan, 2013–14).